New Advances in AI Autonomous Driverless Self-Driving Cars

Practical Advances in Artificial Intelligence (AI) and Machine Learning

Dr. Lance B. Eliot, MBA, PhD

Disclaimer: This book is presented solely for educational and entertainment purposes. The author and publisher are not offering it as legal, accounting, or other professional services advice. The author and publisher make no representations or warranties of any kind and assume no liabilities of any kind with respect to the accuracy or completeness of the contents and specifically disclaim any implied warranties of merchantability or fitness of use for a particular purpose. Neither the author nor the publisher shall be held liable or responsible to any person or entity with respect to any loss or incidental or consequential damages caused, or alleged to have been caused, directly or indirectly, by the information or programs contained herein. Every company is different and the advice and strategies contained herein may not be suitable for your situation.

Copyright © 2017 Lance B. Eliot

All rights reserved. First Edition.

ISBN: 0692048359
ISBN-13: 978-0692048351

DEDICATION

To my incredible son, Michael and my incredible daughter, Lauren.

Forest fortuna adiuvat (from the Latin; good fortune favors the brave).

CONTENTS

Acknowledgments iii

Introduction 1

Chapters

1 Eliot Framework for AI Self-Driving Cars 15
2 Self-Driving Cars Learning from Self-Driving Cars 29
3 Imitation as Deep Learning for Self-Driving Cars 41
4 Assessing Federal Regulations for Self-Driving Cars 53
5 Bandwagon Effect for Self-Driving Cars 65
6 AI Backdoor Security Holes for Self-Driving Cars 75
7 Debiasing of AI for Self-Driving Cars 89
8 Algorithmic Transparency for Self-Driving Cars 97
9 Motorcycle Disentanglement for Self-Driving Cars 107
10 Graceful Degradation Handling of Self-Driving Cars 119
11 AI for Home Garage Parking of Self-Driving Cars 129
12 Motivational AI Irrationality for Self-Driving Cars 139
13 Curiosity as Cognition for Self-Driving Cars 153
14 Automotive Recalls of Self-Driving Cars 165
15 Internationalizing AI for Self-Driving Cars 175
16 Sleeping as AI Mechanism for Self-Driving Cars 187
17 Car Insurance Scams and Self-Driving Cars 199
18 U-Turn Traversal AI for Self-Driving Cars 211
19 Software Neglect for Self-Driving Cars 223

Appendix A: Teaching with this Material 235

Other Self-Driving Car Books by This Author 243

About the Author 249

Addendum 250

i

Lance B. Eliot

ACKNOWLEDGMENTS

I have been the beneficiary of advice and counsel by many friends, colleagues, family, investors, and many others. I want to thank everyone that has aided me throughout my career. I write from the heart and the head, having experienced first-hand what it means to have others around you that support you during the good times and the tough times.

To Warren Bennis, one of my doctoral advisors and ultimately a colleague, I offer my deepest thanks and appreciation, especially for his calm and insightful wisdom and support.

To Mark Stevens and his generous efforts toward funding and supporting the USC Stevens Center for Innovation.

To Lloyd Greif and the USC Lloyd Greif Center for Entrepreneurial Studies for their ongoing encouragement of founders and entrepreneurs.

To Peter Drucker, William Wang, Aaron Levie, Peter Kim, Jon Kraft, Cindy Crawford, Jenny Ming, Steve Milligan, Chis Underwood, Frank Gehry, Buzz Aldrin, Steve Forbes, Bill Thompson, Dave Dillon, Alan Fuerstman, Larry Ellison, Jim Sinegal, John Sperling, Mark Stevenson, Anand Nallathambi, Thomas Barrack, Jr., and many other innovators and leaders that I have met and gained mightily from doing so.

Thanks to Ed Trainor, Kevin Anderson, James Hickey, Wendell Jones, Ken Harris, DuWayne Peterson, Mike Brown, Jim Thornton, Abhi Beniwal, Al Biland, John Nomura, Eliot Weinman, John Desmond, and many others for their unwavering support during my career.

And most of all thanks as always to Lauren and Michael, for their ongoing support and for having seen me writing and heard much of this material during the many months involved in writing it. To their patience and willingness to listen.

Lance B. Eliot

INTRODUCTION

This is a book that provides the newest innovations and the latest Artificial Intelligence (AI) advances about the emerging nature of AI-based autonomous self-driving driverless cars. Via recent advances in Artificial Intelligence (AI) and Machine Learning (ML), we are nearing the day when vehicles can control themselves and will not require and nor rely upon human intervention to perform their driving tasks (or, that <u>allow</u> for human intervention, but only *require* human intervention in very limited ways).

Similar to my three other related books, which I describe in a moment and list the chapters in the Appendix A of this book, I am particularly focused on those advances that pertain to self-driving cars. The phrase "autonomous vehicles" is often used to refer to any kind of vehicle, whether it is ground-based or in the air or sea, and whether it is a cargo hauling trailer truck or a conventional passenger car. Though the aspects described in this book are certainly applicable to all kinds of autonomous vehicles, I am focused more so here on cars.

Indeed, I am especially known for my role in aiding the advancement of self-driving cars, serving currently as the Executive Director of the Cybernetic Self-Driving Cars Institute.. In addition to writing software, designing and developing systems and software for self-driving cars, I also speak and write quite a bit about the topic. This book is a collection of some of my more advanced essays. For those of you that might have seen my essays posted elsewhere, I have updated them and integrated them into this book as one handy cohesive package.

You might be interested in three companion books that I have written that cover additional key innovations and fundamentals about self-driving cars. Those books are entitled **"Advances in AI and Autonomous Vehicles: Cybernetic Self-Driving Cars,"** **"Self-Driving Cars: "The Mother of All AI Projects,"** and **"Innovation and Thought Leadership on Self-Driving Driverless Cars"** (they are all available via Amazon). See Appendix A of this herein book to see a listing of the chapters covered in those three books.

For the introduction here to this book, I am going to borrow my introduction from those companion books, since it does a good job of laying out the landscape of self-driving cars and my overall viewpoints on the topic. The remainder of the book is all new material that does not appear in the companion books.

INTRODUCTION TO SELF-DRIVING CARS

This is a book about self-driving cars. Someday in the future, we'll all have self-driving cars and this book will perhaps seem antiquated, but right now, we are at the forefront of the self-driving car wave. Daily news bombards us with flashes of new announcements by one car maker or another and leaves the impression that within the next few weeks or maybe months that the self-driving car will be here. A casual non-technical reader would assume from these news flashes that in fact we must be on the cusp of a true self-driving car.

Here's a real news flash: We are still quite a distance from having a true self-driving car. It is years to go before we get there.

Why is that? Because a true self-driving car is akin to a moonshot. In the same manner that getting us to the moon was an incredible feat, likewise can it be said for achieving a true self-driving car. Anybody that suggests or even brashly states that the true self-driving car is nearly here should be viewed with great skepticism. Indeed, you'll see that I often tend to use the word "hogwash" or "crock" when I assess much of the decidedly **fake news** about self-driving cars. Those of us on the inside know that what is often reported to the outside is malarkey. Few of the insiders are willing to say so. I have no such hesitation.

Indeed, I've been writing a popular blog post about self-driving cars and hitting hard on those that try to wave their hands and pretend that we are on the imminent verge of true self-driving cars. For many years, I've been known as the AI Insider. Besides writing about AI, I also develop AI software. I do what I describe. It also gives me insights into what others that are doing AI are really doing versus what it is said they are doing.

Many faithful readers had asked me to pull together my insightful short essays and put them into another book, which you are now holding in your hands.

For those of you that have been reading my essays over the years, this collection not only puts them together into one handy package, I also updated the essays and added new material. For those of you that are new to the topic of self-driving cars and AI, I hope you find these essays approachable and informative. I also tend to have a writing style with a bit of a voice, and so you'll see that I am times have a wry sense of humor and also like to poke at conformity.

As a former professor and founder of an AI research lab, I for many years wrote in the formal language of academic writing. I published in referred journals and served as an editor for several AI journals. This writing here is not of the nature, and I have adopted a different and more informal style for these essays. That being said, I also do mention from time-to-time more rigorous material on AI and encourage you all to dig into those deeper and more formal materials if so interested.

I am also an AI practitioner. This means that I write AI software for a living. Currently, I head-up the Cybernetics Self-Driving Car Institute, where we are developing AI software for self-driving cars. I am excited to also report that my son, also a software engineer, heads-up our Cybernetics Self-Driving Car Lab. What I have helped to start, and for which he is an integral part, ultimately he will carry long into the future after I have retired. My daughter, a marketing whiz, also is integral to our efforts as head of our Marketing group. She too will carry forward the legacy now being formulated.

For those of you that are reading this book and have a penchant for writing code, you might consider taking a look at the open source code available for self-driving cars. This is a handy place to start learning how to develop AI for self-driving cars. There are also many new educational courses spring forth.

There is a growing body of those wanting to learn about and develop self-driving cars, and a growing body of colleges, labs, and other avenues by which you can learn about self-driving cars.

This book will provide a foundation of aspects that I think will get you ready for those kinds of more advanced training opportunities. If you've already taken those classes, you'll likely find these essays especially interesting as they offer a perspective that I am betting few other instructors or faculty offered to you. These are challenging essays that ask you to think beyond the conventional about self-driving cars.

THE MOTHER OF ALL AI PROJECTS

In June 2017, Apple CEO Tim Cook came out and finally admitted that Apple has been working on a self-driving car. As you'll see in my essays, Apple was enmeshed in secrecy about their self-driving car efforts. We have only been able to read the tea leaves and guess at what Apple has been up to. The notion of an iCar has been floating for quite a while, and self-driving engineers and researchers have been signing tight-lipped Non-Disclosure Agreements (NDA's) to work on projects at Apple that were as shrouded in mystery as any military invasion plans might be.

Tim Cook said something that many others in the Artificial Intelligence (AI) field have been saying, namely, the creation of a self-driving car has got to be the mother of all AI projects. In other words, it is in fact a tremendous moonshot for AI. If a self-driving car can be crafted and the AI works as we hope, it means that we have made incredible strides with AI and that therefore it opens many other worlds of potential breakthrough accomplishments that AI can solve.

Is this hyperbole? Am I just trying to make AI seem like a miracle worker and so provide self-aggrandizing statements for those of us writing the AI software for self-driving cars? No, it is not hyperbole. Developing a true self-driving car is really, really, really hard to do. Let me take a moment to explain why. As a side note, I realize that the Apple CEO is known for at times uttering hyperbole, and he had previously said for example that the year 2012 was "the mother of all years," and he had said that the release of iOS 10 was "the mother of all releases" – all of which does suggest he likes to use the handy "mother of" expression. But, I assure you, in terms of true self-driving cars, he has hit the nail on the head. For sure.

When you think about a moonshot and how we got to the moon, there are some identifiable characteristics and those same aspects can be applied to creating a true self-driving car. You'll notice that I keep putting the word "true" in front of the self-driving car expression. I do so because as per my essay about the various levels of self-driving cars (see Chapter 3), there are some self-driving cars that are only somewhat of a self-driving car. The somewhat versions are ones that require a human driver to be ready to intervene. In my view, that's not a true self-driving car. A true self-driving car is one that requires no human driver intervention at all. It is a car that can entirely undertake via automation the driving task without any human driver needed. This is the essence of what is known as a Level 5 self-driving car. We are currently at the Level 2 and Level 3 mark, and not yet at Level 5.

Getting to the moon involved aspects such as having big stretch goals, incremental progress, experimentation, innovation, and so on. Let's review how this applied to the moonshot of the bygone era, and how it applies to the self-driving car moonshot of today.

Big Stretch Goal

Trying to take a human and deliver the human to the moon, and bring them back, safely, was an extremely large stretch goal at the time. No one knew whether it could be done. The technology wasn't available yet. The cost was huge. The determination would need to be fierce. Etc. To reach a Level 5 self-driving car is going to be the same. It is a big stretch goal. We can readily get to the Level 3, and we are able to see the Level 4 just up ahead, but a Level 5 is still an unknown as to if it is doable. It should eventually be doable and in the same way that we thought we'd eventually get to the moon, but when it will occur is a different story.

Incremental Progress

Getting to the moon did not happen overnight in one fell swoop. It took years and years of incremental progress to get there. Likewise for self-driving cars. Google has famously been striving to get to the Level 5, and pretty much been willing to forgo dealing with the intervening levels, but most of the other self-driving car makers are doing the incremental route. Let's get a good Level 2 and a somewhat Level 3 going. Then, let's improve the Level 3 and get a somewhat Level 4 going. Then, let's improve the Level 4 and finally arrive at a Level 5. This seems to be the prevalent way that we are going to achieve the true self-driving car.

Experimentation

You likely know that there were various experiments involved in perfecting the approach and technology to get to the moon. As per making incremental progress, we first tried to see if we could get a rocket to go into space and safety return, then put a monkey in there, then with a human, then we went all the way to the moon but didn't land, and finally we arrived at the mission that actually landed on the moon. Self-driving cars are the same way. We are doing simulations of self-driving cars. We do testing of self-driving cars on private land under controlled situations. We do testing of self-driving cars on public roadways, often having to meet regulatory requirements including for example having an engineer or equivalent in the car to take over the controls if needed. And so on. Experiments big and small are needed to figure out what works and what doesn't.

Innovation

There are already some advances in AI that are allowing us to progress toward self-driving cars. We are going to need even more advances. Innovation in all aspects of technology are going to be required to achieve a true self-driving car. By no means do we already have everything in-hand that we need to get there. Expect new inventions and new approaches, new algorithms, etc.

Setbacks

Most of the pundits are avoiding talking about potential setbacks in the progress toward self-driving cars. Getting to the moon involved many setbacks, some of which you never have heard of and were buried at the time so as to not dampen enthusiasm and funding for getting to the moon. A recurring theme in many of my included essays is that there are going to be setbacks as we try to arrive at a true self-driving car. Take a deep breath and be ready. I just hope the setbacks don't completely stop progress. I am sure that it will cause progress to alter in a manner that we've not yet seen in the self-driving car field. I liken the self-driving car of today to the excitement everyone had for Uber when it first got going. Today, we have a different view of Uber and with each passing day there are more regulations to the ride sharing business and more concerns raised. The darling child only stays a darling until finally that child acts up. It will happen the same with self-driving cars.

SELF-DRIVING CARS CHALLENGES

But what exactly makes things so hard to have a true self-driving car, you might be asking. You have seen cruise control for years and years. You've lately seen cars that can do parallel parking. You've seen YouTube videos of Tesla drivers that put their hands out the window as their car zooms along the highway, and seen to therefore be in a self-driving car. Aren't we just needing to put a few more sensors onto a car and then we'll have in-hand a true self-driving car? Nope.

Consider for a moment the nature of the driving task. We don't just let anyone at any age drive a car. Worldwide, most countries won't license a driver until the age of 18, though many do allow a learner's permit at the age of 15 or 16. Some suggest that a younger age would be physically too small to reach the controls of the car. Though this might be the case, we could easily adjust the controls to allow for younger aged and thus smaller stature. It's not their physical size that matters. It's their cognitive development that matters.

To drive a car, you need to be able to reason about the car, what the car can and cannot do. You need to know how to operate the car. You need to know about how other cars on the road drive. You need to know what is allowed in driving such as speed limits and driving within marked lanes. You need to be able to react to situations and be able to avoid getting into accidents. You need to ascertain when to hit your brakes, when to steer clear of a pedestrian, and how to keep from ramming that motorcyclist that just cut you off.

Many of us had taken courses on driving. We studied about driving and took driver training. We had to take a test and pass it to be able to drive. The point being that though most adults take the driving task for granted, and we often "mindlessly" drive our cars, there is a significant amount of cognitive effort that goes into driving a car. After a while, it becomes second nature. You don't especially think about how you drive, you just do it. But, if you watch a novice driver, say a teenager learning to drive, you suddenly realize that there is a lot more complexity to it than we seem to realize.

Furthermore, driving is a very serious task. I recall when my daughter and son first learned to drive. They are both very conscientious people. They wanted to make sure that whatever they did, they did well, and that they did not harm anyone. Every day, when you get into a car, it is probably around 4,000 pounds of hefty metal and plastics (about two tons), and it is a lethal weapon. Think about it. You drive down the street in an object that weighs two tons and with the engine it can accelerate and ram into anything you want to hit. The damage a car can inflict is very scary. Both my children were surprised that they were being given the right to maneuver this monster of a beast that could cause tremendous harm entirely by merely letting go of the steering wheel for a moment or taking your eyes off the road.

In fact, in the United States alone there are about 30,000 deaths per year by auto accidents, which is around 100 per day. Given that there are about 263 million cars in the United States, I am actually more amazed that the number of fatalities is not a lot higher. During my morning commute, I look at all the thousands of cars on the freeway around me, and I think that if all of them decided to go zombie and drive in a crazy maniac way, there would be many people dead. Somehow, incredibly, each day, most people drive relatively safely. To me, that's a miracle right there. Getting millions and millions of people to be safe and sane when behind the wheel of a two ton mobile object, it's a feat that we as a society should admire with pride.

So, hopefully you are in agreement that the driving task requires a great deal of cognition. You don't' need to be especially smart to drive a car, and we've done quite a bit to make car driving viable for even the average dolt. There isn't an IQ test that you need to take to drive a car. If you can read and write, and pass a test, you pretty much can legally drive a car. There are of course some that drive a car and are not legally permitted to do so, plus there are private areas such as farms where drivers are young, but for public roadways in the United States, you can be generally of average intelligence (or less) and be able to legally drive.

This though makes it seem like the cognitive effort must not be much. If the cognitive effort was truly hard, wouldn't we only have Einstein's that could drive a car? We have made sure to keep the driving task as simple as we can, by making the controls easy and relatively standardized, and by having roads that are relatively standardized, and so on. It is as though Disneyland has put their Autopia into the real-world, by us all as a society agreeing that roads will be a certain way, and we'll all abide by the various rules of driving.

A modest cognitive task by a human is still something that stymies AI. You certainly know that AI has been able to beat chess players and be good at other kinds of games. This type of narrow cognition is not what car driving is about. Car driving is much wider. It requires knowledge about the world, which a chess playing AI system does not need to know. The cognitive aspects of driving are on the one hand seemingly simple, but at the same time require layer upon layer of knowledge about cars, people, roads, rules, and a myriad of other "common sense" aspects. We don't have any AI systems today that have that same kind of breadth and depth of awareness and knowledge.

As revealed in my essays, the self-driving car of today is using trickery to do particular tasks. It is all very narrow in operation. Plus, it currently assumes that a human driver is ready to intervene. It is like a child that we have taught to stack blocks, but we are needed to be right there in case the child stacks them too high and they begin to fall over. AI of today is brittle, it is narrow, and it does not approach the cognitive abilities of humans. This is why the true self-driving car is somewhere out in the future.

Another aspect to the driving task is that it is not solely a mind exercise. You do need to use your senses to drive. You use your eyes a vision sensors to see the road ahead. You vision capability is like a streaming video, which your brain needs to continually analyze as you drive. Where is the road? Is there a pedestrian in the way? Is there another car ahead of you? Your senses are relying a flood of info to your brain. Self-driving cars are trying to do the same, by using cameras, radar, ultrasound, and lasers. This is an attempt at mimicking how humans have senses and sensory apparatus.

Thus, the driving task is mental and physical. You use your senses, you use your arms and legs to manipulate the controls of the car, and you use your brain to assess the sensory info and direct your limbs to act upon the controls of the car. This all happens instantly. If you've ever perhaps gotten something in your eye and only had one eye available to drive with, you suddenly realize how dependent upon vision you are. If you have a broken foot with a cast, you suddenly realize how hard it is to control the brake pedal and the accelerator. If you've taken medication and your brain is maybe sluggish, you suddenly realize how much mental strain is required to drive a car.

An AI system that plays chess only needs to be focused on playing chess. The physical aspects aren't important because usually a human moves the chess pieces or the chessboard is shown on an electronic display. Using AI for a more life-and-death task such as analyzing MRI images of patients, this again does not require physical capabilities and instead is done by examining images of bits.

Driving a car is a true life-and-death task. It is a use of AI that can easily and at any moment produce death. For those colleagues of mine that are developing this AI, as am I, we need to keep in mind the somber aspects of this. We are producing software that will have in its virtual hands the lives of the occupants of the car, and the lives of those in other nearby cars, and the lives of nearby pedestrians, etc. Chess is not usually a life-or-death matter.

Driving is all around us. Cars are everywhere. Most of today's AI applications involve only a small number of people. Or, they are behind the scenes and we as humans have other recourse if the AI messes up. AI that is driving a car at 80 miles per hour on a highway had better not mess up. The consequences are grave. Multiply this by the number of cars, if we could put magically self-driving into every car in the USA, we'd have AI running in the 263 million cars. That's a lot of AI spread around. This is AI on a massive scale that we are not doing today and that offers both promise and potential peril.

There are some that want AI for self-driving cars because they envision a world without any car accidents. They envision a world in which there is no car congestion and all cars cooperate with each other. These are wonderful utopian visions.

They are also very misleading. The adoption of self-driving cars is going to be incremental and not overnight. We cannot economically just junk all existing cars. Nor are we going to be able to affordably retrofit existing cars. It is more likely that self-driving cars will be built into new cars and that over many years of gradual replacement of existing cars that we'll see the mix of self-driving cars become substantial in the real-world.

In these essays, I have tried to offer technological insights without being overly technical in my description, and also blended the business, societal, and economic aspects too. Technologists need to consider the non-technological impacts of what they do. Non-technologists should be aware of what is being developed.

We all need to work together to collectively be prepared for the enormous disruption and transformative aspects of true self-driving cars. We all need to be involved in this mother of all AI projects.

WHAT THIS BOOK PROVIDES

What does this book provide to you? It introduces many of the key elements about self-driving cars and does so with an AI based perspective. I weave together technical and non-technical aspects, readily going from being concerned about the cognitive capabilities of the driving task and how the technology is embodying this into self-driving cars, and in the next breath I discuss the societal and economic aspects.

They are all intertwined because that's the way reality is. You cannot separate out the technology per se, and instead must consider it within the milieu of what is being invented and innovated, and do so with a mindset towards the contemporary mores and culture that shape what we are doing and what we hope to do.

WHY THIS BOOK

I wrote this book to try and bring to the public view many aspects about self-driving cars that nobody seems to be discussing.

For business leaders that are either involved in making self-driving cars or that are going to leverage self-driving cars, I hope that this book will enlighten you as to the risks involved and ways in which you should be strategizing about how to deal with those risks.

For entrepreneurs, startups and other businesses that want to enter into the self-driving car market that is emerging, I hope this book sparks your interest in doing so, and provides some sense of what might be prudent to pursue.

For researchers that study self-driving cars, I hope this book spurs your interest in the risks and safety issues of self-driving cars, and also nudges you toward conducting research on those aspects.

For students in computer science or related disciplines, I hope this book will provide you with interesting and new ideas and material, for which you might conduct research or provide some career direction insights for you.

For AI companies and high-tech companies pursuing self-driving cars, this book will hopefully broaden your view beyond just the mere coding and development needed to make self-driving cars.

For all readers, I hope that you will find the material in this book to be stimulating. Some of it will be repetitive of things you already know. But I am pretty sure that you'll also find various eureka moments whereby you'll discover a new technique or approach that you had not earlier thought of. I am also betting that there will be material that forces you to rethink some of your current practices.

I am not saying you will suddenly have an epiphany and change what you are doing. I do think though that you will reconsider or perhaps revisit what you are doing.

For anyone choosing to use this book for teaching purposes, please take a look at my suggestions for doing so, as described in the Appendix. I have found the material handy in courses that I have taught, and likewise other faculty have told me that they have found the material handy, in some cases as extended readings and in other instances as a core part of their course (depending on the nature of the class).

In my writing for this book, I have tried carefully to blend both the practitioner and the academic styles of writing. It is not as dense as is typical academic journal writing, but at the same time offers depth by going into the nuances and trade-offs of various practices.

The word "deep" is in vogue today, meaning getting deeply into a subject or topic, and so is the word "unpack" which means to tease out the underlying aspects of a subject or topic. I have sought to offer material that addresses an issue or topic by going relatively deeply into it and make sure that it is well unpacked.

Finally, in any book about AI, it is difficult to use our everyday words without having some of them be misinterpreted. Specifically, it is easy to anthropomorphize AI. When I say that an AI system "knows" something, I do not want you to construe that the AI system has sentience and "knows" in the same way that humans do. They aren't that way, as yet. I have tried to use quotes around such words from time-to-time to emphasize that the words I am using should not be misinterpreted to ascribe true human intelligence to the AI systems that we know of today. If I used quotes around all such words, the book would be very difficult to read, and so I am doing so judiciously. Please keep that in mind as you read the material, thanks.

COMPANION BOOKS

If you find this material of interest, you might want to also see my other three books on self-driving cars, entitled:

- **"Innovation and Thought Leadership on Self-Driving Driverless Cars" by Dr. Lance Eliot**

- **"Advances in AI and Autonomous Vehicles: Cybernetic Self-Driving Cars" by Dr. Lance Eliot**

- ***"Self-Driving Cars: The Mother of All AI Projects"* by Dr. Lance Eliot**

All of the above three books are available on Amazon and at other booksellers.

CHAPTER 1
ELIOT FRAMEWORK FOR AI SELF-DRIVING CARS

CHAPTER 1
ELIOT FRAMEWORK FOR AI SELF-DRIVING CARS

When I give presentations about self-driving cars and teach classes on the topic, I have found it helpful to provide a framework around which the various key elements of self-driving cars can be understood and organized (see diagram at the end of this chapter). The framework needs to be simple enough to convey the overarching elements, but at the same time not so simple that it belies the true complexity of self-driving cars. As such, I am going to describe the framework here and try to offer in a thousand words (or more!) what the framework diagram itself intends to portray.

The core elements on the diagram are numbered for ease of reference. The numbering does not suggest any kind of prioritization of the elements. Each element is crucial. Each element has a purpose, and otherwise would not be included in the framework. For some self-driving cars, a particular element might be more important or somehow distinguished in comparison to other self-driving cars. You could even use the framework to rate a particular self-driving car, doing so by gauging how well it performs in each of the elements of the framework.

I will describe each of the elements, one at a time. After doing so, I'll discuss aspects that illustrate how the elements interact and perform during the overall effort of a self-driving car.

At the Cybernetic Self-Driving Car Institute, we use the framework to keep track of what we are working on, and how we are developing software that fills in what is needed to achieve Level 5 self-driving cars.

D-01: Sensor Capture

Let's start with the one element that often gets the most attention in the press about self-driving cars, namely, the sensory devices for a self-driving car.

On the framework, the box labeled as D-01 indicates "Sensor Capture" and refers to the processes of the self-driving car that involve collecting data from the myriad of sensors that are used for a self-driving car. The types of devices typically involved are listed, such as the use of mono cameras, stereo cameras, LIDAR devices, radar systems, ultrasonic devices, GPS, IMU, and so on.

These devices are tasked with obtaining data about the status of the self-driving car and the world around it. Some of the devices are continually providing updates, while others of the devices await an indication by the self-driving car that the device is supposed to collect data. The data might be first transformed in some fashion by the device itself, or it might instead be fed directly into the sensor capture as raw data. At that point, it might be up to the sensor capture processes to do transformations on the data. This all varies depending upon the nature of the devices being used and how the devices were designed and developed.

D-02: Sensor Fusion

Imagine that your eyeballs receive visual images, your nose receives odors, your ears receive sounds, and in essence each of your distinct sensory devices is getting some form of input. The input befits the nature of the device. Likewise, for a self-driving car, the cameras provide visual images, the radar returns radar reflections, and so on. Each device provides the data as befits what the device does.

At some point, using the analogy to humans, you need to merge together what your eyes see, what your nose smells, what your ears hear, and piece it all together into a larger sense of what the world is all about and what is happening around you. Sensor fusion is the action of taking the singular aspects from each of the devices and putting them together into a larger puzzle.

Sensor fusion is a tough task. There are some devices that might not be working at the time of the sensor capture. Or, there might some devices that are unable to report well what they have detected. Again, using a human analogy, suppose you are in a dark room and so your eyes cannot see much. At that point, you might need to rely more so on your ears and what you hear. The same is true for a self-driving car. If the cameras are obscured due to snow and sleet, it might be that the radar can provide a greater indication of what the external conditions consist of.

In the case of a self-driving car, there can be a plethora of such sensory devices. Each is reporting what it can. Each might have its difficulties. Each might have its limitations, such as how far ahead it can detect an object. All of these limitations need to be considered during the sensor fusion task.

D-03: Virtual World Model

For humans, we presumably keep in our minds a model of the world around us when we are driving a car. In your mind, you know that the car is going at say 60 miles per hour and that you are on a freeway. You have a model in your mind that your car is surrounded by other cars, and that there are lanes to the freeway. Your model is not only based on what you can see, hear, etc., but also what you know about the nature of the world. You know that at any moment that car ahead of you can smash on its brakes, or the car behind you can ram into your car, or that the truck in the next lane might swerve into your lane.

The AI of the self-driving car needs to have a virtual world model, which it then keeps updated with whatever it is receiving from the sensor fusion, which received its input from the sensor capture and the sensory devices.

D-04: System Action Plan

By having a virtual world model, the AI of the self-driving car is able to keep track of where the car is and what is happening around the car. In addition, the AI needs to determine what to do next. Should the self-driving car hit its brakes? Should the self-driving car stay in its lane or swerve into the lane to the left? Should the self-driving car accelerate or slow down?

A system action plan needs to be prepared by the AI of the self-driving car. The action plan specifies what actions should be taken. The actions need to pertain to the status of the virtual world model. Plus, the actions need to be realizable.

This realizability means that the AI cannot just assert that the self-driving car should suddenly sprout wings and fly. Instead, the AI must be bound by whatever the self-driving car can actually do, such as coming to a halt in a distance of X feet at a speed of Y miles per hour, rather than perhaps asserting that the self-driving car come to a halt in 0 feet as though it could instantaneously come to a stop while it is in motion.

D-05: Controls Activation

The system action plan is implemented by activating the controls of the car to act according to what the plan stipulates. This might mean that the accelerator control is commanded to increase the speed of the car. Or, the steering control is commanded to turn the steering wheel 30 degrees to the left or right.

One question arises as to whether or not the controls respond as they are commanded to do. In other words, suppose the AI has commanded the accelerator to increase, but for some reason it does not do so. Or, maybe it tries to do so, but the speed of the car does not increase. The controls activation feeds back into the virtual world model, and simultaneously the virtual world model is getting updated from the sensors, the sensor capture, and the sensor fusion. This allows the AI to ascertain what has taken place as a result of the controls being commanded to take some kind of action.

By the way, please keep in mind that though the diagram seems to have a linear progression to it, the reality is that these are all aspects of the self-driving car that are happening in parallel and simultaneously. The sensors are capturing data, meanwhile the sensor fusion is taking place, meanwhile the virtual model is being updated, meanwhile the system action plan is being formulated and reformulated, meanwhile the controls are being activated.

This is the same as a human being that is driving a car. They are eyeballing the road, meanwhile they are fusing in their mind the sights, sounds, etc., meanwhile their mind is updating their model of the world around them, meanwhile they are formulating an action plan of what to do, and meanwhile they are pushing their foot onto the pedals and steering the car. In the normal course of driving a car, you are doing all of these at once. I mention this so that when you look at the diagram, you will think of the boxes as processes that are all happening at the same time, and not as though only one happens and then the next.

They are shown diagrammatically in a simplistic manner to help comprehend what is taking place. You though should also realize that they are working in parallel and simultaneous with each other. This is a tough aspect in that the inter-element communications involve latency and other aspects that must be taken into account. There can be delays in one element updating and then sharing its latest status with other elements.

D-06: Automobile & CAN

Contemporary cars use various automotive electronics and a Controller Area Network (CAN) to serve as the components that underlie the driving aspects of a car. There are Electronic Control Units (ECU's) which control subsystems of the car, such as the engine, the brakes, the doors, the windows, and so on.

The elements D-01, D-02, D-03, D-04, D-05 are layered on top of the D-06, and must be aware of the nature of what the D-06 is able to do and not do.

D-07: In-Car Commands

Humans are going to be occupants in self-driving cars. In a Level 5 self-driving car, there must be some form of communication that takes place between the humans and the self-driving car. For example, I go into a self-driving car and tell it that I want to be driven over to Disneyland, and along the way I want to stop at In-and-Out Burger. The self-driving car now parses what I've said and tries to then establish a means to carry out my wishes.

In-car commands can happen at any time during a driving journey. Though my example was about an in-car command when I first got into my self-driving car, it could be that while the self-driving car is carrying out the journey that I change my mind. Perhaps after getting stuck in traffic, I tell the self-driving car to forget about getting the burgers and just head straight over to the theme park. The self-driving car needs to be alert to in-car commands throughout the journey.

D-08: VX2 Communications

We will ultimately have self-driving cars communicating with each other, doing so via V2V (Vehicle-to-Vehicle) communications. We will also have self-driving cars that communicate with the roadways and other aspects of the transportation infrastructure, doing so via V2I (Vehicle-to-Infrastructure).

The variety of ways in which a self-driving car will be communicating with other cars and infrastructure is being called V2X, whereby the letter X means whatever else we identify as something that a car should or would want to communicate with. The V2X communications will be taking place simultaneous with everything else on the diagram, and those other elements will need to incorporate whatever it gleans from those V2X communications.

D-09: Deep Learning

The use of Deep Learning permeates all other aspects of the self-driving car. The AI of the self-driving car will be using deep learning to do a better job at the systems action plan, and at the controls activation, and at the sensor fusion, and so on.

Currently, the use of artificial neural networks is the most prevalent form of deep learning. Based on large swaths of data, the neural networks attempt to "learn" from the data and therefore direct the efforts of the self-driving car accordingly.

D-10: Tactical AI

Tactical AI is the element of dealing with the moment-to-moment driving of the self-driving car. Is the self-driving car staying in its lane of the freeway? Is the car responding appropriately to the controls commands? Are the sensory devices working?

For human drivers, the tactical equivalent can be seen when you watch a novice driver such as a teenager that is first driving. They are focused on the mechanics of the driving task, keeping their eye on the road while also trying to properly control the car.

D-11: Strategic AI

The Strategic AI aspects of a self-driving car are dealing with the larger picture of what the self-driving car is trying to do. If I had asked that the self-driving car take me to Disneyland, there is an overall journey map that needs to be kept and maintained.

There is an interaction between the Strategic AI and the Tactical AI. The Strategic AI is wanting to keep on the mission of the driving, while the Tactical AI is focused on the particulars underway in the driving effort. If the Tactical AI seems to wander away from the overarching mission, the Strategic AI wants to see why and get things back on track. If the Tactical AI realizes that there is something amiss on the self-driving car, it needs to alert the Strategic AI accordingly and have an adjustment to the overarching mission that is underway.

D-12: Self-Aware AI

Very few of the self-driving cars being developed are including a Self-Aware AI element, which we at the Cybernetic Self-Driving Car Institute believe is crucial to Level 5 self-driving cars.

The Self-Aware AI element is intended to watch over itself, in the sense that the AI is making sure that the AI is working as intended. Suppose you had a human driving a car, and they were starting to drive erratically. Hopefully, their own self-awareness would make them realize they themselves are driving poorly, such as perhaps starting to fall asleep after having been driving for hours on end. If you had a passenger in the car, they might be able to alert the driver if the driver is starting to do something amiss. This is exactly what the Self-Aware AI element tries to do, it becomes the overseer of the AI, and tries to detect when the AI has become faulty or confused, and then find ways to overcome the issue.

D-13: Economic

The economic aspects of a self-driving car are not per se a technology aspect of a self-driving car, but the economics do indeed impact the nature of a self-driving car. For example, the cost of outfitting a self-driving car with every kind of possible sensory device is prohibitive, and so choices need to be made about which devices are used. And, for those sensory devices chosen, whether they would have a full set of features or a more limited set of features.

We are going to have self-driving cars that are at the low-end of a consumer cost point, and others at the high-end of a consumer cost point. You cannot expect that the self-driving car at the low-end is going to be as robust as the one at the high-end. I realize that many of the self-driving car pundits are acting as though all self-driving cars will be the same, but they won't be. Just like anything else, we are going to have self-driving cars that have a range of capabilities. Some will be better than others. Some will be safer than others. This is the way of the real-world, and so we need to be thinking about the economics aspects when considering the nature of self-driving cars.

D-14: Societal

The societal aspects also impact the technology of self-driving car. For example, the famous Trolley Problem involves what choices should a self-driving car make when faced with life-and-death matters. If the self-driving car is about to either hit a child standing in the roadway, or instead ram into a tree at the side of the road and possibly kill the humans in the self-driving car, which choice should be made?

We need to keep in mind the societal aspects will underlie the AI of the self-driving car. Whether we are aware of it explicitly or not, the AI will have embedded into it various societal assumptions.

D-15: Innovation

I included the notion of innovation into the framework because we can anticipate that whatever a self-driving car consists of, it will continue to be innovated over time. The self-driving cars coming out in the next several years will undoubtedly be different and less innovative than the versions that come out in ten years hence, and so on.

Framework Overall

For those of you that want to learn about self-driving cars, you can potentially pick a particular element and become specialized in that aspect. Some engineers are focusing on the sensory devices. Some engineers focus on the controls activation. And so on. There are specialties in each of the elements.

Researchers are likewise specializing in various aspects. For example, there are researchers that are using Deep Learning to see how best it can be used for sensor fusion. There are other researchers that are using Deep Learning to derive good System Action Plans. Some are studying how to develop AI for the Strategic aspects of the driving task, while others are focused on the Tactical aspects.

A well-prepared all-around software developer that is involved in self-driving cars should be familiar with all of the elements, at least to the degree that they know what each element does. This is important since whatever piece of the pie that the software developer works on, they need to be knowledgeable about what the other elements are doing.

NEW ADVANCES IN AI AUTONOMOUS DRIVERLESS SELF-DRIVING CARS

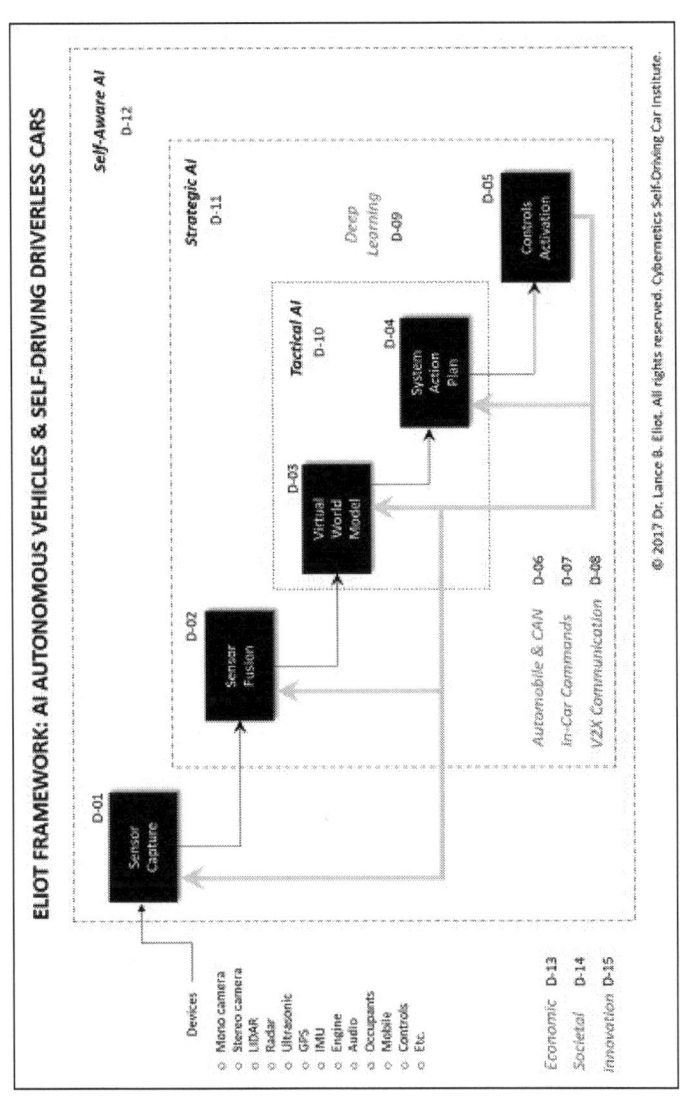

CHAPTER 2
SELF-DRIVING CARS LEARNING FROM SELF-DRIVING CARS

CHAPTER 2

SELF-DRIVING CARS LEARNING FROM SELF-DRIVING CARS

When my daughter started to drive, I did my fatherly duty and sat in the passenger seat while providing gentle tips and suggestions on how to drive a car (ranging from putting the car into gear to strategies of freeway traversal). For anyone that has ever aided a novice driver, you know how terrifying it can be. There you are, urging to keep their foot on the brake, and the next thing you know they are stomping on the accelerator and the car is leaping forward. You watch as they struggle to make those corners or stop fully at stop signs.

After each such session, I'd get out of the car with weak knees, but at least I knew that I was doing my part to help her become a full-fledged driver and do so with some insight about the nature of the driving task. I'll add that today, a few years later, she's a wonderful driver, and as a passenger I sit back and enjoy the ride (though, perhaps a bit fast for my taste).

Next, when my son then came along and started to drive, I was better prepared and felt that I could do an even better job at coaching and guiding about how to drive a car. There is a twist though to this that I had not anticipated. Turns out that he had been learning from my daughter, and so he was already somewhat up the learning curve on driving a car. My daughter, being my eldest, did not have an older sibling to help teach her, but my son, realizing that his older sister could help, had enlisted her assistance. Who knew this would happen? I suppose that I should have guessed it would, since this same pattern had occurred for other things in life, whereby she would for example take a history class and then later on he'd take the same history class, and they'd compare notes and such.

In the realm of human learning, these are examples of an "expert" teaching a "novice" (that's me teaching my children), along with an example of a "novice" teaching a fellow "novice" (that's my daughter teaching my son). Now, you can argue about whether my daughter was still a novice when she was helping to teach my son, since she by then had a few years of driving experience under her belt. Let's perhaps say she was a "semi-expert" driver, somewhat above a novice but still not quite what one might consider an expert driver. I suppose you could even contest whether I am an "expert" driver, which, I use that moniker simply due to having been a driver for many years and so somewhat think I am an expert at driving. Of course, if you compare me to say an Indie race car driver then I'm no longer an expert per se on a relative basis, and would rightfully agree that the race car driver is more of an expert than me.

Both of my children could have tried to learn on their own. I'd say they both did in the following sense – they each had watched my driving and had tried to glean what they could about driving by the manner in which I drive a car. This is a kind of self-learning, whereby there isn't explicit instruction provided to the learner. Instead, the learner uses observation to try and learn the nature of a task. In some respects, your children will do this without being overtly aware, since they while being passengers in a car are soaking up the driving experience anyway. They subconsciously likely notice how fast you drive, how hard your stops are, and otherwise can by osmosis gain some semblance of the driving task. But, they can also be explicitly aware, such as the times that my son or daughter would notice that I suddenly swerved the car to avoid debris in the roadway, and they would then ask what had happened, why I had responded the way I did, etc. This was part of the subtle but indeed focused self-learning about this task.

What does this have to do with self-driving cars?

The answer is straightforward, namely that self-driving cars can and ought to be learning not only by being programmed but also by learning from other self-driving cars. I'll let that soak in for a moment.

It's a key area of research and practice that we're doing at the Cybernetic Self-Driving Car Institute.

There are robots in the manufacturing realm that are programmed to do a particular task. Let's say that we want a robot arm to grasp a cup made of glass, and then we want the arm to swing over to a second position and place the cup safely onto a pedestal. Programmers can write instructions in specific robotic control programming languages that will step-by-step indicate what the robot arm is supposed to do. First step, swing the arm over to the cup. Second step, move the robot hand to the cup. Third step, grasp the cup. Fourth step, while grasping the cup then swing to the pedestal. Fifth step, while positioned over the pedestal then let go of the cup. Something like that would be the series of instructions.

We are pushing the envelope further in robotics by saying that maybe we don't need to always be there to program a robot, and instead setup the robot to be able to learn a task by itself. In this manner, the robot can be readily "re-programmed" to do lots of tasks and it does not take a human programmer to be able to reprogram the robot.

One notion is to establish overall parameters and then let the robot via trial-and-error try to ascertain how to do a task. This is sometimes referred to as a "robot learning in the raw" (the use of the word "raw" suggests that this type of learning is going to be often slow and ponderous, since it is based on a trial-and-error approach). For example, a robotic arm that was "learning" to grasp a cup had made over 800,000 attempts, and along the way it "realized" that grasping a soft object versus a hard object required differing amounts of grasping strength and pressure. The robot had not been programmed directly to softly grasp a soft object, and strongly grasp a strong object, but instead it had essentially deduced this by thousands of attempts at grasping various objects. This robot had used a relatively large-scale convolutional neural network (CNN), and the artificial neural network had found these patterns over the course of the trial-and-error series.

Please note that I am wanting to be careful in my use of the word "learn" when it comes to robotics. The nature and type of learning that we are having robots do is not necessarily the same as humans do learning, and in fact we are still not fully sure how the human brain indeed learns things. So, I ask that you keep in mind that I am trying to avoid anthropomorphizing robots and assume that you are aware that I am aware that they aren't doing robotic learning as we humans do learning per se.

Let's suppose we are able to have a robot arm that successfully learns how to grasp an object. Could we have that robot then "teach" another robot to do the same thing? Or, alternatively, could we have one robot that "learns" from another robot about how to do that same thing? Well, whether you think this is a good idea for society and mankind, which some are worried it sounds like a doomsday scenario, it is certainly something of keen interest to see if it can be done. This is the latest focus for many in the robotics field.

We are doing the same with self-driving cars. Rather than having to program a self-driving car to be able to do the driving task, let's have a self-driving car teach another self-driving car about how to drive. Or, alternatively, have a self-driving car learn from another self-driving car. The self-driving car that is teaching another self-driving car would presumably be doing so with the awareness that it is doing teaching. This is akin to my having taught my daughter and son how to drive. I was sitting in the passenger seat and knew that I was teaching, and they knew that I was teaching them. In contrast, the circumstance of them watching me drive, and subtly picking up clues about the driving task, that's a case of them learning about driving but without necessarily my even knowing that I was "teaching" them – I was merely driving.

Here are the ways in which self-driving cars can learn:

a) Self-driving car learns from the collective wisdom of other self-driving cars

b) Self-driving car learns by programmatic insertion of knowledge from other self-driving cars

c) Self-driving car learns by passive observational learning of other self-driving cars

d) Self-driving car learns by active shared learning with other self-driving cars

We're making use of each of these methods at our Lab.

I'll address here each of these approaches briefly. Note that there is nothing mutually exclusive regarding these approaches, and as such you should keep in mind that a self-driving car could make use of one or more of these, and do so at the same time or at different points in time. This is not a one shoe size fits all aspect.

a) Self-driving car learns from the collective wisdom of other self-driving cars

This is well exemplified by the existing Tesla approach of learning for self-driving cars. A centralized collective is being used whereby the Tesla cars on-the-road are reporting into the collective global system with various aspects about their respective driving experiences. The collective can then share that "wisdom" down into the self-driving cars. This is done by the over-the-air updates that the Tesla cars are ready to receive.

For a collective approach, you should keep in mind that not everything that is being individually learned is necessarily of value or even appropriate for other self-driving cars to learn from. Suppose one car happens to learn that to navigate a bumpy road off highway 40 is done by going slowly for the first 90 yards and then doing an acute turn to the left. It is hard to imagine that this rather idiosyncratic aspect is going to provide any particular value to all the other cars in the collective. On the other hand, suppose that a car has devised a better way to parallel park a car, in this case the collective could gain great value if the learned task is something that can be applied on a widespread basis.

b) Self-driving car learns by programmatic insertion of knowledge from other self-driving cars

For many self-driving cars, we are using artificial neural networks for purposes of machine learning and deep learning. If you've got a large-scale neural network that underlies say the freeway driving prowess of a certain model of self-driving car, the question arises whether you could take that neural network and plug it into another self-driving car so that it suddenly would have that same knowledge about how to drive on freeways.

Right now, there are numerous models for neural networks and thus it is difficult to share any piecemeal aspects of one neural network with another self-driving car. It is like one self-driving car that is based on VHS and the other based on Beta (historical note, these were famous standards factions during the early days of video tapes).

Furthermore, we don't yet have any across the board standards of what a neural network consists of, and so trying to extract a portion of one and insert into another is problematic. It would be akin to trying to do brain surgery on a human and take part of the brain of one person and surgically place it into another person's brain. We aren't at a juncture where the human brain is well enough understood to do something like this. For artificial neural networks, in a somewhat crude analogous manner, we also cannot yet just carve out one chunk and place it into another artificial neural network such that we could transplant the neural knowledge from one robotic type system to another.

c) Self-driving car learns by passive observational learning of other self-driving cars

We've been having one self-driving car watch other self-driving cars, and try to glean from passive observations any tricks or techniques for driving a car. This is similar to what I was saying earlier about my children watching me drive a car. In the case of a self-driving car, the learner self-driving car does not necessarily let the other self-driving car even know that it is being observed. Instead, the self-driving car that is learning is just watching and trying to figure out whatever it can figure out on its own.

This makes sense too in that once we have lots of self-driving cars on the roadways, we might as well have them learning by observing each other. I'll also point out that the self-driving car can be learning by watching human driven cars too. There is nothing keeping the learner self-driving car from observing both human driven cars and also other self-driving cars. You could suggest that it is "better" for a self-driving car to learn from another self-driving car, since they are both of the same ilk. I get that idea, but at the same time the techniques being used by humans to drive a car offer plentiful insights too.

One important aspect to keep in mind about the passive observational learning mode is that the self-driving car learning in this fashion might learn the wrong thing. Back to my children and their watching me, suppose that each time that I got on the freeway and it was bumper-to-bumper traffic that I drove right up to the edge of being on the bumper of the car ahead of me. This is not a very safe way to drive. But, my children might not realize the dangerous aspect of such driving, and thus inadvertently learn how to drive in a rather unsafe manner. Any self-driving car that is learning by passive observation needs to have some added means to gauge whether the learning itself is worthwhile or not.

d) Self-driving car learns by active shared learning with other self-driving cars

In this mode, a self-driving car is engaged in a connection with another self-driving car, and the self-driving cars share what they know. This is a peer-to-peer form of learning. One self-driving car might be the teacher and be pretty much doing a one-way of sharing knowledge about driving over to the "novice" self-driving car. Or, they might both have aspects worthy of sharing with each other. Suppose one self-driving car is adept at driving in the city, while the other self-driving car is adept at driving on the open highways. The city driving self-driving car could share what it knows, and so the other self-driving car now has awareness about city driving, and likewise the open highway driving self-driving car shares what it knows with the city driving self-driving car.

They can share in various ways. One aspect of sharing is their respective collected sensory data. The city driving self-driving car has lots of data about city landscapes and so it can quickly pump over to the other self-driving car aspects about what city roads, signs, buildings, etc. are like. They can also potentially share their neural networks (though keep in mind my caveats earlier mentioned herein), and other AI code.

For all of the above approaches, there are aspects about learning that need to be kept at the forefront of doing any kind of self-driving car to self-driving car learning.

Here's some key points:

1) Must be capable of learning

Most of the self-driving cars of today are being built with the idea that human programmers are essentially teaching the self-driving cars what they need to know. We need to make sure that self-driving cars have a learning capacity built into them. Without which, they will be somewhat stagnant and wholly dependent upon being human programmed.

2) Must be willing to learn

Besides having the capacity to learn, a self-driving car must be "willing" to learn in the sense that it is able to open itself to learning, when so appropriate. If the self-driving car is busy trying to drive and it is being tasked with some tough driving circumstance, that's likely not the best time to turn-on the learning mode.

3) Must be available to learn

If a self-driving car is trying to convey to another self-driving car that is has some handy driving tip to share, the other self-driving car must have the capacity to learn and must be willing to learn and must be available to learn. For example, suppose the self-driving car is parked at the side of the road and waiting to be commanded by a human to undertake a driving task. This might be a good time for the self-driving car to learn something, perhaps doing so as other self-driving cars whisk past. Or, maybe while parked next to another self-driving car. I suppose you can imagine this as though it is two chauffeurs waiting for their driving gigs, each sharing some tips about driving.

4) Must be able to judge what is learned

There is a real danger that anything learned might be wrong or might be only usable in certain circumstances. A self-driving car cannot allow itself to blindly learn something. It needs to have a means to gauge whether or not what is learned has value and when to make use of it. This is especially important not only by inadvertently learning something that is amiss, but also as a means of security. If a self-driving car is willing to blindly learn anything, a nefarious person could have their self-driving car communicate to another self-driving car that it should go drive off a cliff. The self-driving car that is open to learning must be able to judge the appropriateness of what it is learning.

5) Must be able to apply learnings properly

Besides learning something from other self-driving cars, a self-driving car needs to know how to apply it correctly. Suppose a self-driving car that can accelerate from 0 to 60 miles per hour in 2 seconds tries to teach another self-driving car that it can escape from dangerous situations by rapid acceleration. But suppose that the other self-driving car is sluggish and it goes from 0 to 60 miles per hour in 8 seconds. The notion that rapid acceleration is a driving technique needs to be applied accordingly to the learning self-driving car. It might not be able to use that technique or might need to adapt it according to its own ways and capabilities.

This whole topic of self-driving cars learning from other self-driving cars is an exciting means of pushing forward on getting self-driving cars to become true self-driving cars (i.e. reaching the vaunted Level 5). Perhaps a Level 4 self-driving car can get to become a Level 5 self-driving car by learning from some other self-driving car that is already at Level 5. This could tremendously speed-up getting self-driving cars up the learning curve.

Does this also portend that we might have self-driving cars that become sentient beings and overrun humans? I don't think so. For those that believe we are on the verge of a Frankenstein by making use of learning within self-driving cars, I just don't see that this is a likely outcome. Of course, I realize some will say that I am blind to this aspect and that I am leading us toward the emergence of Skynet (per the movie "Terminator"). If so, all I can say is oops.

CHAPTER 3

IMITATION AS DEEP LEARNING FOR SELF-DRIVING CARS

CHAPTER 3

IMITATION AS DEEP LEARNING SELF-DRIVING CARS

I was driving on a freeway that I rarely go onto, and the traffic was completely snarled with pure bumper-to-bumper slowness as far as the eye could see.

Besides listening to the traffic reports on the radio, my mind was clawing at finding a means to somehow get around or through this freeway road blockage. Didn't want to get off the freeway, even if it might be faster to get to my destination, mainly because the areas off the freeway are known for high crime rates and best to be avoided. I could maybe sprout wings on my car and try to fly over the thousands of cars, but the sprouting wings are in the same place as my long awaited personal jet pack (hey, I thought we were all supposed to have jet packs by now!).

I noticed up ahead a car that was desperately trying to get from the fast lane all the way over to the upcoming freeway exit. The driver was squeezing into each successive lane to the right, pushing into those lanes and acting nearly like a maniac. I assumed that the driver had suddenly realized that their desired exit was coming and rather than having gradually gotten over to it, the driver was now in a panic. The car barely made it to the exit and I figured that's the last I would ever see of that crazy car.

To my surprise, in a few minutes, I saw the same exact car up ahead of me on the freeway. What kind of magic trick was this? Did I dream that the car had exited? Can the driver make their car appear and disappear at will? I was now interested in this particular car. Well, it could also be the boredom of being stuck in inching along traffic.

Anyway, I noticed that the car had pushed over into the second lane from the right, thus he wasn't in the so-called slow lane, and he wasn't yet in the so-called fast lane. There was an opening in the freeway in that particular lane and I noticed that the driver seemed to have anticipated it would be there.

In this instance, the freeway was bending to the left, and the inner most lanes were now jammed, but that second lane from the right had a clear passage for about a quarter mile. I also looked at my GPS and realized that the prior exit that the car had used was actually both an exit and an entrance onto the freeway. The driver had used it to slip ahead of the rest of the traffic, by entering into it as though exiting the freeway, but then using the extended portion that came back onto the freeway, and got ahead of the rest of the cars on the freeway.

I deduced that this was a driver that knew this freeway well. The driver was aware of the various tricks to get around the traffic bog. One method was to use an exit that was also an entrance, and thus jump ahead of the freeway traffic. Another was to know the bends of the freeway and anticipate whether the inner lanes or outer lanes would be the most likely to have the best flow. I am guessing that the driver probably drove this stretch dozens of times a month and knew the in's and out's of it. If you've ever seen the famous movie "Groundhog Day" you'll know what I mean when I say that the driver has studied this over and over, finding ways to optimize their driving journey.

Unless I have mental telepathy, I realized that I would not have any direct means of knowing what that driver knows. There was one thing I could do, though, and that was to imitate the other driver. In other words, follow along and try to do the same things that the other driver is doing, and presumably therefore gain the same advantages. I might not even know why for example that I am suddenly to get into one lane or another, but if I imitate what the other driver is doing then there was a good chance that I too would be optimizing my driving. Would I follow the other driver over a cliff? No, that I wouldn't do. Anything that the other driver did that seemed legal and reasonable, I was willing to try. It worked out pretty well and I was able to shave a lot of time off my trip.

What does this have to do with self-driving cars?

It has to do with using imitation or mimicry as a deep learning technique for self-driving cars. At the Cybernetic Self-Driving Car Institute, we are researching and putting into practice the use of mimicry for self-driving cars and find that it is a novel and promising approach for improving self-driving car capabilities.

Before we get into the technical details, I'd like to remind you of the quote by Confucius about imitation: "By three methods we may learn wisdom: First, by reflection, which is noblest; Second, by imitation, which is easiest; and third by experience, which is the bitterest."

I'll say right now that imitation is not as easy as it might seem. Yes, you can readily copy what someone else is doing, but if you do so blindly you can end-up in trouble. As mentioned before, I was not going to go over a cliff simply because the other driver went off a cliff. Maybe the other driver knew that going off a cliff was safe to do, or maybe the timing of going off the cliff if done just right would be OK, but on the other hand maybe the other driver made a mistake and going over the cliff was going to lead to their death. With imitation, you need to add judgement, else the end result could be disastrous.

A self-driving car has sensors that allow it to scan the scene around it and detect where other vehicles are. Most of the time, the self-driving car is just trying to avoid hitting those other cars. The AI prevents the self-driving car from switching lanes into another car, or avoids hitting a car up ahead by slowing down the self-driving car. A good self-driving car is also observing other cars to predict what they might do next. If a car to the left of the self-driving car is weaving in and out of its lane, it could be a sign that the driver is drunk. As such, the self-driving car might want to move over to another lane, or attempt to stay behind or get way in front of the suspected drunken driver.

Another perspective on what to do about other cars involves considering imitating them. A self-driving car does this somewhat already by the standard technique of car following. In car following, the self-driving car detects a car directly ahead of it, and then matches the speed and braking of that car. If the car ahead speeds up, the self-driving car speeds up. If the car ahead slows down, the self-driving car slows down. When the car ahead taps its brakes, a good self-driving car will start to tap its brakes too. This is all a form of imitation, though relatively simplistic.

It is simplistic is several ways. One is that the self-driving car is not especially paying attention to the specific car ahead, but more like any car ahead of it. Thus, if the car ahead suddenly switches to another lane, the algorithm for car following usually just latches onto whatever car is next ahead of the self-driving car. The self-driving car is not tracking the car that was previously ahead of it. That car is now lost among a sea of cars. Instead, the self-driving car is merely spotting whichever car is ahead of it. There is no relationship per se between the self-driving car and that car ahead that was being followed. It was transitory and just being used as a vehicle for car following while in the lane that the self-driving car is in.

What we are doing at our Lab is actually tracking other cars, and using the AI to figure out whether other cars that are on-the-road with the self-driving car might provide some imitation worthy practices that the self-driving car can leverage. We assign labels to all the surrounding cars and then track them for as long as the self-driving car can still spot them. Over time, some of those cars go out of the range of the sensors, and thus the self-driving car assumes they are no longer trackable, but might be tracked again later on.

Those cars that have gone beyond tracking scope can re-enter into the tracking scope. Similar to my story about the car that exited and then came back onto the freeway ahead of me, the self-driving car AI realizes that cars will come and go, and that they might reappear. Sometimes this can be because the other car pulls a stunt like the driver that appeared to exit and came back onto the freeway. In other cases, the other car has gone outside the viable range of the sensors and so it is no longer readily detected. For example, if a car goes past my car at 80 miles per hour, and I am doing 50 miles per hour, it will soon enough get so far ahead of me that no use of my eyes will still see it. Likewise, for a self-driving car, another car can go beyond the range of the cameras and radar, seemingly therefore no longer being trackable.

I think we all know though that cars that go outside our scope can readily come back into our scope. The car that zoomed past me at 80 miles per hour might soon up ahead encounter snarled traffic. The car gets stuck at the back of the pack. I come along at my 50 miles per hour, eventually catching up with that car, and now am at the back of the pack with that same car. The other car was in my scope, then outside my scope, and now back into my scope. A self-driving car can track cars in the same manner, realizing that the cars will enter into and exit from scope, during the driving journey.

How do you know that it was the same car? The obvious approach involves reading the license plate of the other car. This is handy, but often not feasible. The other car might only be seen from a distance or be blocked by other intervening cars. You cannot assume that you'll always be able to detect the license plate. Just as humans look for other clues, so does the self-driving car. It detects aspects such as the type of car, make and model, color of the car, design and shape of the car, etc.

We also include personalized characteristics such as whether the car has stickers on the back, or a broken tail light, or even if it is muddied and maybe has some prominent dents. Or a roof rack. And so on. Now, admittedly, you can have more than one car that looks the same as another car, and so you need to be cautious in concluding that a car being tracked, once lost, and then seemingly reappears, will indeed be that same exact car. It could be a car that is similar. We use probabilities to assign the likelihood that the same car was the one being tracked.

On my morning commute, I leave my house each day at around the same time and travel on the same streets and freeways to get to work. Over the course of my hour or longer commute, I tend to see many of the same cars, day after day. This is not happenstance. Those cars are presumably trying to get to work in a geographic area roughly the same as me and so it makes sense that they would each day be going along the same overall route. If I leave earlier or later, I tend not to see those cars. It is a window of time that dictates that I see them again and again. I recognize their cars, without paying any attention to their license plates. There's that bright blue BMW that likes to go fast, and there's that red Chevy Bolt that holds up traffic. I know them by what they look like.

Notice that I also know those cars by what they do. I've observed them over time. I have seen how they drive in traffic. This takes us to the next aspect of imitation for self-driving cars. Besides spotting a car and tracking it, the next aspect involves making sense of the tracking. What is the other car doing? Does it exhibit any patterns of driving?

Once the self-driving car is aware of these other trackable cars, and been identifying patterns of their behavior, the next step involves ascertaining whether there is anything worthwhile to mimic.

We divide imitation into two major categories, tactical imitation and strategic imitation. Let's take a look at each of these.

TACTICAL IMITATION

In tactical imitation, the AI of the self-driving car is looking for any small sized imitation carveouts that might be worth considering doing.

Here's some aspects taken into consideration:

a) Specific maneuver

Has the other car been able to do a specific maneuver that might be worth also doing? For example, suppose there is a sharp curve ahead. The car ahead has seemed to be a good driver, and so if the car as it takes the curve hugs the inside of the road, perhaps this is a tactical maneuver that the self-driving car should also do.

b) Contextual memory

The self-driving car maintains a context for the maneuver. For example, the hugging of the inside of the road worked for a particular sharp curve, and so maybe that's the only circumstance that warrants doing the hug. Realizing the context is crucial to deciding whether to imitate and also when to imitate.

c) Transitory

Cars do lots of things, some stupid, some smart. Tracking of other cars will result in mainly aspects that aren't worthy of remembering. There is a ton of throw away. It's those few tidbits that the AI is searching for. When I was on the freeway and saw the car ahead of my get into the second lane from the right and then had an opening, I didn't also tell you about the dozens of other cars around me that were doing all sorts of twists and turns. The volume of tracking other cars is huge, and you need to have the AI find that worthwhile needle in the haystack.

d) Immediacy

In the tactical use of mimicry, the self-driving car either opts to mimic something that has just occurred or it does not, and the moment then vanishes. In essence, there is a time decay of the mimicking. It's pretty much a monkey-see and monkey-do kind of situation. The AI has to work fast enough to ascertain whether the mimicry is worthy and if so whether the time window to do so is still open or not. Keep in mind that it takes time to process the volume of data about the cars around it, and so time is a crucial element in all of this.

STRATEGIC IMITATION

In strategic imitation, the AI of the self-driving car is looking for either tactical imitations that might have lifelong value, or larger sized imitation carveouts that might be worth considering doing permanently.

Here's some aspects taken into consideration:

a) Generalizable maneuvers

Remember that during a tactical mimicry, it's all about the specific context, such as perhaps the self-driving car mimicked a car that was getting onto the freeway via an onramp and realized that rapid acceleration to the very end of the onramp was a tactic worthy to imitate. This rapid acceleration might work for that particular onramp on that particular day and at that particular time, but then not be viable in any other circumstances.

Or, it might be that doing a rapid acceleration on an onramp until its end would be handy in situations that are befitting that maneuver. The strategic imitation tries to generalize from specific maneuvers and figure out when those maneuvers can otherwise be applied.

b) Larger constructs

In the tactical realm, each maneuver is essentially a standalone. In the strategic realm, the AI is trying to piece together perhaps several maneuvers into a larger picture. When I had seen the driver that went off the freeway and come back on, and then also saw that the driver cleverly got into lane that was going to open up due to a curve, it provided more than just those singular tactics. It provided a pattern of driving behavior about how to make my way through this freeway during crowded times.

c) Saved up for future use

A strategic perspective takes the viewpoint that even if a particular tactic cannot be immediately mimicked, it can be stored for future use. Maybe getting to that exit to come back onto the freeway is out of the reach of the self-driving car when it first witnesses it. But, by remembering it, and upon the next such instance of being on that freeway, it can now mimic that other car, even though that other car is no longer around. It is a delayed learned-mimicry or imitation.

IMITATION ASPECTS

For those that believe in Neurolinguistics Programming (NLP), they are all about modeling your human behavior after the behavior of other people, especially of successful people. That's kind of what we are trying to do for self-driving cars. Have self-driving cars be able to model their behavior after the behavior of other cars, whether human driven vehicles or other self-driving cars.

There is a theory of other minds which recently in biological studies showed that there are mirror neurons in the ventral pre-motor area of monkeys. It is believed that perhaps these neurons are used to undertake imitation or mimicry. Imitation seems to be a extremely popular behavior among most animals. Humans of course do so.

You might even recall the Charles Caleb Cotton quote: "Imitation is the sincerest form of flattery." Self-driving cars can improve their capabilities by leveraging what seems to be an innate feature of most living organisms, the ability to imitate. Imitation is not something though done by the foolhardy. Self-driving cars and their AI need to realize that imitating another car that drives off a cliff is not the proper use of mimicry.

CHAPTER 4
ASSESSING FEDERAL REGULATIONS FOR SELF-DRIVING CARS

CHAPTER 4
ASSESSING FEDERAL REGULATIONS FOR SELF-DRIVING CARS

There is an ongoing debate about the role of government regulations regarding self-driving cars. At times, the debate is well measured. On other occasions, it is quite heated and accompanied by outbursts, finger pointing, and otherwise acrimonious behavior.

Whenever there is a new innovation, this same kind of debate takes place. In that sense, there is nothing unusual about a debate of this nature taking place. We should expect it to take place. One might say that it is the norm of the yin and yang that occurs for innovations and technology, involving society trying to wrestle with how to best cope with something new.

Often, the core of the debate comes down to socio-political beliefs. Depending upon your perspective about the purpose and role of government, you will tend to land on one side or another of the debate. It also depends on the stakes involved. If it is a high stakes innovation, the odds are that there will be greater polarization of viewpoints.

In the United States, we typically wrestle with these top-level contentions:

USA competitiveness

Pro. If the USA regulatory environment becomes overly restrictive on an innovation, this could mean that then the USA will fall behind other countries and so no longer remain competitive. Furthermore, the

USA might lose out on being the first to market or not be considered the owner of the innovation, all of which imply that the USA will be second fiddle. This could suggest too that the USA is no longer innovative and have other repercussions internationally.

Con. The counter-argument to this is that if the USA allows an innovation to proceed unfettered it could allow for something that is dangerous to move into the marketplace. Perhaps in the haste to get to market first, safety will be compromised and the public will be endangered. The USA could not only suffer but also end-up releasing something amiss onto the world at large (this is the so-called Frankenstein model).

Both of the above positions have merit. It is hard at times to know which position is the "best" in a given circumstance. We can't know the future and can only predict the future, thus, for any innovation, it is not clear cut how it is going to turn out.

With self-driving cars, there are those that are saying that the USA needs to be at the forefront of the advent of self-driving cars. This is then used to suggest that any regulatory restrictions need to be reined-in, or else the USA auto makers of self-driving cars will be suppressed in terms of moving forward or moving forward with rapidity.

On the other hand, clearly self-driving cars involve life-and-death matters. This is an innovation that will be on our roadways and has the potential to harm and kill. There's no debating that aspect. Others though point out that self-driving cars will potentially save lives, emphasizing the number of car related deaths today and make the assumption that those deaths will no longer occur once self-driving cars are on the roads.

This aspect then takes us to the next top-level contention, the balance between federal regulations and state regulations.

Federal versus State regulations

Pro. Presumably, our USA system of government desires that the states have as much power over their efforts as feasible, countered by certain aspects for which the federal or collective viewpoint should at times override. For example, if every state enacts regulations that are disparate, it might make it very difficult for an innovation to take hold as it must somehow meet so many differing requirements. The federal role aids in ensuring that there is consistency across the board and a level playing field.

Con. States though need to presumably protect their own, and if they see an innovation in a different manner, they should have the ability to treat it in that manner. To what degree should the federal role intercede in that which a state sees as crucial to their state? This has been a tension for as long as the country has been in existence.

In terms of self-driving cars, currently there are 21 states that have to-date passed regulations pertaining to self-driving cars. Here's the list, shown in alphabetical order: Alabama, Arkansas, California, Colorado, Connecticut, Florida, Georgia, Illinois, Louisiana, Michigan, New York, Nevada, North Carolina, North Dakota, Pennsylvania, South Carolina, Tennessee, Texas, Utah, Virginia, Vermont, and Washington D.C. Most of the remaining states are in the midst of considering or passing self-driving car regulations.

One argument is that these myriad of state-based regulations are a spotty patchwork of regulations that are unwieldy for those making self-driving cars. It is as though there are too many cooks in the kitchen. That's part of the basis for the federal efforts toward creating self-driving car regulations.

There are those though that also are questioning whether the effort to craft federal self-driving car regulations are really doing so as a ploy instigated by the auto makers to try and override the states. There is concern that the federal regulations will be a watered-down version that allows for unsafe aspects of self-driving cars. It also raises once again the tension between state preferences and federal preferences.

This discussion and debate about self-driving has been ongoing for now several years. The general public is not particularly aware of these debates since it has been pretty much occurring between the regulators, the auto makers, and special interest groups. Recently, after months of discussion by the US House of Representatives, a new bill on self-driving cars was passed, and this now has widened the public attention to the topic.

Another bill is currently being considered in the Senate. At some point, assuming that there are indeed two bills created, there will need to be a resolving of the two and then have it land on the President's desk. As such, it is still early to be predicting what the final bill will be, and whether or not it will ultimately become law. Nonetheless, it is useful to closely look at the House bill that was passed. I next provide passages verbatim from the bill, and provide commentary about it.

At the Cybernetic Self-Driving Car Institute, we are keeping close tabs on the state and federal regulations, and also analyzing what other countries are doing about regulating self-driving cars too. I'd say that all of us have a stake in the topic of self-driving cars, and as such, I am hopeful that the general public will become further engaged and contact their respective state and federal representatives to indicate input to these matters. This is one of the biggest innovations of our times and will have a huge impact on economies, society, and how we live our lives. It's important.

Section 1.

Excerpt: "This Act may be cited as the "Safely Ensuring Lives Future Deployment and Research In Vehicle Evolution Act" or the "SELF DRIVE Act"."

You have to give credit to our regulators that they like to come up with catchy names for things. Here, they are calling the House bill the SELF DRIVE act, and did some reverse engineering to come up with the letters standing for Safely Ensuring Lives Future (SELF) and Deployment and Research In Vehicle Evolution (DRIVE). Does not roll off the tongue. Stilted. But anyway, we get the idea.

A rose is a rose by any other name.

Section 2.

Excerpt: "The purpose of this Act is to memorialize the Federal role in ensuring the safety of highly automated vehicles as it relates to design, construction, and performance, by encouraging the testing and deployment of such vehicles."

This portion provides an indicated purpose for the bill.

Note that the wording refers to "highly automated vehicles" which is generally considered a preferred terminology over self-driving cars, and allows for a wider latitude of coverage of types of automated vehicles. Notice too that the life cycle of these vehicles is mentioned, which clarifies that the bill is not just about say the design, or just about the construction, but about all aspects of the life cycle.

Indeed, as worded, the bill is more so about the testing of and deployment of these vehicles, which some would say is wise to allow for less restrictions about how it comes to be (i.e., design, construction), and instead focus more so on what the end result will be (by doing testing and regulating deployment). There are some though that believe the regulations should be more extensive and cover more overtly the upfront side of things (design and construction), which, presumably, would then lead to more likely safer vehicles as based on the endpoint of testing and deployment.

Section 3.

Excerpt: "No State or political subdivision of a State may maintain, enforce, prescribe, or continue in effect any law or regulation regarding the design, construction, or performance of highly automated vehicles, automated driving systems, or components of automated driving systems unless such law or regulation is identical to a standard prescribed under this chapter."

This is a part of the bill that has drawn ire and caused heartburn for the states. It essentially says that the states nor any local regulatory body within a state can put in place their own self-driving car laws unless those laws are the same as the laws stated in this bill. Welcome to the tension between the feds and the states.

Excerpt: "Nothing in this subsection may be construed to prohibit a State or a political subdivision of a State from maintaining, enforcing, prescribing, or continuing in effect any law or regulation regarding registration, licensing, driving education and training, insurance, law enforcement, crash investigations, safety and emissions inspections, congestion management of vehicles on the street within a State or political subdivision of a State, or traffic unless the law or regulation is an unreasonable restriction on the design, construction, or performance of highly automated vehicles, automated driving systems, or components of automated driving systems."

In this passage, the federal regulation somewhat does a give-back to the states in terms of what is covered about self-driving cars from a state perspective. But, this is not entirely a full give-back and you can see that the wording of "…unless the law or regulation is an unreasonable restriction" is purposely included.

Expect to see a legal battle ensure between the states and the federal government on what the meaning of "unreasonable" is. Hope the courts are ready for this.

Section 4.

Excerpt: "Not later than 24 months after the date of the enactment of this section, the Secretary of Transportation shall issue a final rule requiring the submission of safety assessment certifications regarding how safety is being addressed by each entity developing a highly automated vehicle or an automated driving system. Such rule shall include: (A) a specification of which entities are required to submit such certifications; (B) a clear description of the relevant test results, data, and other contents required to be submitted by such entity, in order to demonstrate that such entity's vehicles are likely maintain safety, and function as intended and contain fail safe features, to be included in such certifications; and (C) a specification of the circumstances under which such certifications are required to be updated or resubmitted."

Here, this is an indication that the rules about attesting to safety are going to be derived over time and no later than two years from the enactment of this bill. Some would say that allowing for up to two years is a bit odd, given the fast pace of this innovation. The bill though does indicate what should happen in the interim, which provides some guidance, but there are some that believe that this not sufficient and we need to know sooner what the true final rules will be.

Section 8.

Excerpt: "Not later than 3 years after the date of enactment of this Act, the Secretary of Transportation shall complete research to determine the most effective method and terminology for informing consumers for each highly automated vehicle or a vehicle that performs partial driving automation about the capabilities and limitations of that vehicle. The Secretary shall determine whether such information is based upon or includes the terminology as defined by SAE International in Recommended Practice Report J3016 (published September 20 2016) or whether such description should include alternative terminology."

This passage has to do with making sure that consumers are aware of what they are getting when they buy a self-driving car. It is akin to how we now have auto makers letting us know how many miles per gallon the car will typically get. For self-driving cars, there are so many variations as to what a self-driving car is and has, it could be handy to have some kind of standards that are used and also that the consumer would need to be notified as to which of those standards the self-driving car abided to.

One criticism here is that the "not later than 3 years" might be letting the horses out of the barn, and that the time frame needs to be much sooner so as to ensure that there are standards in place before self-driving cars are being sold to consumers.

Section 12.

Excerpt: "A manufacturer may not sell, offer for sale, introduce or deliver for introduction in interstate commerce, or import into the United States, any highly automated vehicle, vehicle that performs partial driving automation, or automated driving system unless the manufacturer has developed a privacy plan that includes the following: (1) A written privacy plan with respect to the collection, use, sharing, and storage of information about vehicle owners or occupants collected by a highly automated vehicle, vehicle that performs partial driving automation, or automated driving system. Such policy shall include the following: (A) The practices of the manufacturer with respect to the way that information about vehicle owners or occupants is collected, used, shared, or stored. (B) The practices of the manufacturer with respect to the choices offered to vehicle owners or occupants regarding the collection, use, sharing, and storage of such information. (C) The practices of the manufacturer with respect to the data minimization, detection, and retention of information about vehicle owners or occupants. (D) The practices of the manufacturer with respect to extending its privacy plan to the entities it shares such information with. (2) A method for providing notice to vehicle owners or occupants about the privacy policy. (3) If information about vehicle owners or occupants is altered or combined so that the information can no longer reasonably be linked to the highly automated vehicle, vehicle that performs partial driving automation, or automated driving system from which the information is retrieved, the vehicle owner, or occupants, the manufacturer is not required to include the process or practices regarding that information in the privacy policy. (4) If information about an occupant is anonymized or encrypted the manufacturer is not required to include the process or practices regarding that information in the privacy policy."

This passage is about privacy aspects for consumers. It is handy and especially since there are state regulations about self-driving cars that either don't mention privacy as an explicit topic or just assume that other existing privacy laws will cover self-driving cars. That being said, there are some that are not convinced that this privacy portion has enough teeth in it.

Other Aspects.

I am not going to walk you through all of the aspects of the bill, but encourage you to consider taking a look at it and getting further up-to-speed.

Some salient points of contention include:

Appears to exempt auto makers from various safety standards that are not presumably applicable to self-driving cars and yet are applicable to traditional cars (this seems like a questionable carve out to many).

Appears to provide overreaching authority to the federal government about self-driving cars by grabbing the design and performance, and denies the states their due, yet it does seem to still allow the states to decide if they want to permit self-driving cars to be on the roads in their state.

Appears to allow to remain intact that the states can regulate the driver of a vehicle, but, in the case of self-driving cars, and if there is not a human driver, does that mean that the states then are no longer regulating the driver (human or AI), or does it mean that they could enact legislation that covers the AI that is driving the car ("the driver").

Is this bill too sweet for the auto makers? Some say so. Meanwhile, some auto makers say it doesn't go far enough for their needs to proceed with rapidity toward self-driving cars. Is it onerous on the auto makers?

Various consumer and safety groups say that it weakens safety considerations and opens the gate for auto makers to jam self-driving cars onto consumers with reckless abandon. If so, we'll see injuries and deaths from self-driving cars that might well kill-off the self-driving car momentum, besides also becoming a menace to society.

There is concern expressed that the bill does not address commercial vehicles. Who and what is going to regulate those self-driving trucks and other such commercial vehicles? They would seem to need regulations as much as do conventional self-driving cars.

Whether you agree or disagree with the contents of the House bill, it provides at least a place to start debating more widely and openly the issues surrounding the emergence of self-driving cars. We all have a stake in this high-stake game.

In the range from no regulations to onerous regulations, presumably we can find something within that spectrum that will achieve the advent of self-driving cars but do so without self-driving cars becoming killing machines that lack appropriate safety and security provisions.

CHAPTER 5
BANDWAGON EFFECT FOR SELF-DRIVING CARS

CHAPTER 5
BANDWAGON EFFECT FOR SELF-DRIVING CARS

Have you hopped onto the bandwagon for self-driving cars? If not, maybe you ought to think about doing so. The FOMO (fear of missing out) alone should be enough to get you motivated to jump in.

Some people say that the self-driving car bandwagon is just a fad. According to the fad theory, once the self-driving car turns out to be a dud, meaning that no such thing is feasible, everyone will be upset, and then everyone will move onto the next big thing. Under this hypothesis, those that made investments into self-driving cars (or the making of self-driving cars) are going to have lost their shirts. It will be like the so-called Internet bubble that burst and left a lot of stockholders bereft of profits.

There are those that say the opposite, namely that the self-driving car is the next miracle to save mankind. It will herald incredible changes in societal norms, in economies, in lives. Having a car, or at least having access to a car, will now become within the grasp of all people, rich or poor, civilized or uncivilized. The self-driving car will change what we do, when we do it, how we live, and otherwise be nearly as big as the invention of fire.

Which is it?

Well, whichever way the self-driving car ends-up, one thing for sure is that right now it still has its allure at top peak. Even if you think that this is merely the currently most hyped tech item on the hype curve, keep in mind that it is still indeed being touted. Whether you sincerely believe in self-driving cars or not, there are those that are finding ways to at least ride the curve up, and then trying to make sure they don't get hurt if the curve then falls downward.

There's the false positive, namely the false belief that self-driving cars are going to do well and so thereby be supportive of self-driving cars. That's pretty much a somewhat safe bet, if you hedge your bets.

There's the false negative, namely the false believe that self-driving cars are going to tank, and so either ignore them or even campaign against them. This is a somewhat risky bet, since no one usually likes doomsayers (they just seem to be depressing), and also if the naysayers are wrong then they miss out on the upside. As an example, I've known many that had an opportunity to invest in Apple during the early days, and at the time these naysayers were insistent that Apple wasn't going anywhere. Today, they look out their window of their townhouse apartment and wish they were living on a remote island with their own mansion, which they could have had if they had put their money into Apple stock in the early days.

Now, there are some situations where you'd be kind of foolish not to get onto the self-driving car bandwagon, particularly if you could use it to your advantage. I'll use as a case in point the circumstance of the former CEO of Ford, Mark Fields, whom seemed to have gotten hung by his rather milk-toast support for self-driving cars.

Mark Fields had been in the auto industry for most of his entire career. He was a long-time Ford employee. He was the CEO for three years and then in mid-2017 got booted out of the head job. What happened? Depending upon which version you prefer, there are different reasons for the gigantic job loss.

The version we'll go with involves that during his tenure as CEO, he made what many considered to be a half-hearted effort to go toward self-driving cars. He infamously came out and had said that Ford would not be the first to come out with self-driving cars, and indeed added fuel to that fire by saying that Ford didn't even want to be first.

This would normally be a prudent thing to say. He was merely trying to suggest that self-driving cars are still an unknown and that as a conservative company that wants to make sure it does things right that it wanted to make sure that self-driving cars are perfected before Ford brings them out. Certainly seems like a rationale thing to say. Very mindful of consumers. Also, as a large company with a massive base of shareholders, one could say that he had a duty to protect them from potentially crazy fads. His approach seemed to be measured, allowing him to say that Ford was doing something about self-driving cars, but not betting the farm on it. Let those wild tech companies stick their necks out on self-driving cars. Ford owes its stockholders and its car owners to be prudent about where it focuses its time and energy.

Yes, that might seem like a solid and sensible outlook, but Ford got hammered. During his tenure, the stock had slipped 40% in value. Some viewed that the lack of eagerness for self-driving cars showed how backward and lumbering Ford was. It just seemed to reinforce the belief that major car makers are stodgy and stuck in the past. It was akin to taxi companies that wanted to act like Uber and Lfyt weren't much and so no real need to take them seriously. Their lunch has gotten eaten by these ridesharing services.

Once Mark was ejected from Ford, they put Jim Hackett in his place. Jim has essentially no particular auto industry experience, but had been brought into Ford a year earlier to head-up their self-driving car efforts. Bill Ford even came out and emphasized that Jim was a transformative leader that would take Ford to where it needs to go in the future. For many, this was a clear cut indication that Ford believes in self-driving cars and will be doing its upmost toward self-driving cars.

So, however you believe things played out at Ford, one aspect that seems relatively apparent was that Mark had not gotten onto the self-driving car bandwagon. What could he have done? He could have been gushing about how it was the future, even if maybe back at the ranch only giving it half-hearted attention. In this case, his own words seemed to get him hung. As a major auto maker, the tsunami of interest in self-driving cars was squarely in his industry, and he sidestepped it. As we can see, he did so at his own peril.

We've gradually seen that most of the car makers wised up that whether the self-driving car is going to make it or not, it's a much safer bet to go along with the idea that it might. The public perception of auto makers that don't jump onto the bandwagon is just so severely limiting that it makes little sense not to join the bandwagon. The good news for those on the bandwagon is that since nearly everyone else has gotten onto it too, if the self-driving car does hit a rut and goes sideways, at least you can say that you aren't the only one and that it caught everyone by surprise.

Recently, Fiat announced it is joining a self-driving car partnership that had already been formed between BMW and Intel. This is a clever way to get onto the self-driving car bandwagon. Associate yourself with other seemingly progressive companies that are pursuing self-driving cars with great vigor. Doing so prevents your stockholders from carping at you that you aren't doing something about self-driving cars. You can point to the partnership and say, look at these great partners we've mated with.

Fiat Chrysler had already dipped a toe into the self-driving car realm by providing the Pacific hybrid minivan to Google for Waymo's self-driving car efforts. This helped get them a seat on the bandwagon, but many still perceived that they were only half-on and half-off. What to do? If they launched into their own self-driving car effort it could be quite expensive. And, as I say, if self-driving cars aren't going to become real, it could be a lot of dough down the drain. Thus, the partnership approach gets them further into the self-driving car realm but does so by hedging their bet. They are unlikely to make a big lotto ticket type win, on the other hand they aren't going to get beat-up about the head for not being into self-driving cars.

Fiat Chrysler's CEO said it well: "Joining this cooperation will enable FCA to directly benefit from the synergies and economies of scale that are possible when companies come together with a common vision and objective." In other words, we are hedging our bets by distributing the risk, and even though we aren't likely to get a home run by having developed the self-driving car ourselves and have a lock on it, we will at least be in the swimming pool with everyone else and have a good chance of being there when (if) it takes off.

It seems rather obvious that any company in the auto industry should be joining the self-driving car bandwagon.

What about other industries?

Of course, ride sharing companies are getting onto the self-driving car bandwagon. They have to do so. They are considered progressives due to how they leveraged high-tech to get to their now explosive and disruptive position. If they won't embrace the next big high-tech thing, they would be considered really out-of-touch. They would be considered heads-in-the-sand. They live and die by tech.

This also applies to the high-tech companies.

For example, Apple has been swinging back and forth about how much it is into self-driving cars. The early indications were that they were going to do a skunk works effort and come out with an amazing self-driving car that would turn all other self-driving cars into shame. Think of it like surprising the market with the iPhone and putting other mobile phones to shame. But, then Apple seemed to have wavered from that be-there-first perspective, and we've seen that instead they are more aimed toward providing tech for self-driving cars, rather than becoming a kind of auto maker themselves. Nothing wrong with that, by the way, and I am merely pointing out how hard it is to decide where on the self-driving car bandwagon you should be.

We've seen that Amazon realizes the value of the self-driving car bandwagon. What better way to make that last mile to reaching the consumer? Use a self-driving car. They already got such incredible publicity out of the idea of drones that fly and deliver your Amazon goods, so why not also try for a self-driving car.

We'll gradually see others get onto the self-driving car bandwagon, including companies that maybe at first surprise you. One of my favorites is the current experiment being done by Domino's.

When you order pizza from Domino's, they were one of the first major pizza delivery firms to exploit the use of mobile apps and really did well by doing so. Consumers could load-up the Domino's mobile app, order their pizza, and then watch as the pizza moved from stage-to-stage of reaching them. The app would tell you that the pizza was being made. Then, the pizza is on the delivery vehicle. Then, the pizza is nearing your location. Clever and caused a lot of consumers to feel like Domino's was hip, using high-tech in a business that presumably is only about making pizzas.

Domino's is at it again, and this time they are aiming at self-driving cars. They are doing an experiment with Ford to outfit the Ford Fusion

Hybrid self-driving car with special pizza containers. The pizza remains nice and hot inside the container. You order a pizza and receive via the mobile app a numeric delivery code. When the self-driving car pulls up to your place, you go out to the vehicle, enter your delivery code on a pad outside of the car, the back window opens, you grab your pizza box, and voila you've been served by a self-driving car.

Note that the experiment is only right now in Ann Arbor, Michigan, so if you are rushing right this moment to order a Domino's pizza and if you don't live in Ann Arbor than a regular pizza delivery person in some downtrodden rusty car is going to be delivering your pizza, not a shiny new self-driving car, sorry.

They are touting this as an ethnographic research project, one that is trying to figure out how to best deliver pizza and whether people are willing to have it done via a self-driving car. You might wonder why they care. Well, if soon we are going to have self-driving cars, and right now if Domino's relies on pizza delivering humans, what is Domino's going to do? I suppose you could say that they should just put a delivery person into the self-driving car, one that doesn't even need to know how to drive a car (that might help to keep their labor costs lower), and then the self-driving car can take the delivery person to the place where the pizza is to be delivered.

This does bring up the side aspect that will people be willing to leave their home or apartment to walk out to a self-driving car to get their pizza? If you are in your pajamas, you are probably not going to want to make that walk. If you are half-drunk, you are probably not going to want to make that walk. We'll need to see how many are willing to not have the pizza actually delivered directly to their door.

Right now, the whole thing is part research and part cleverly devised public relations. I tip my hat to them. This is the perfect example of being on the self-driving car bandwagon. The cost to do the experiment is low. The public relations is high. They get tons of attention for the effort, and maybe it produces something and maybe not. Either way, it shows Domino's as being progressive, which is exactly what it wants to do and needs to do to keep those fickle pizza eaters coming back. It makes Ford look progressive, and turns those millennials that like the hipness of Domino's into thinking that old-timer Ford aka "my parent's car company" is maybe a firm they should consider buying a car from.

You might be saying to yourself, hey, Lance, I'm not an auto maker, I'm not a ride sharing service, I'm not an Amazon, I'm not a Domino's, so how do I get onto the self-driving car bandwagon?

Glad you asked.

There are other ways.

If you are a software developer, you can recast your skill set into the self-driving car marketplace. This is growing rapidly. Unfortunately, you don't have much time to get there. The self-driving car industry is scrambling to develop software and right now they need the developers. If it takes you a year or two to reskill, it is likely by then that the mania will have subsided.

If you are doing research in almost anything that could be allied with self-driving cars, you would be wise to consider making something about your research that applies to self-driving cars. We're seeing more research monies flowing over to work on self-driving cars. It's mainly in the AI field and the engineering fields, but there is also some heading toward the social sciences, economics, and other fields that can help us figure out what impact self-driving cars are going to have on us.

For any kind of bandwagon, especially in high-tech, you need to consider where you want to be. Here's the possibilities:

a) Be on the bandwagon

b) Be thinking about being on the bandwagon but not yet made the leap

c) Got onto the bandwagon but did so too early and now are burned out

d) Got onto the bandwagon but did so belatedly and missed the relish of it

e) Hate the bandwagon and refuse to get onto it

f) Were runover by the bandwagon and wish you had seen it coming

g) Didn't even know the bandwagon existed

h) Other

Whether you love or hate the idea of self-driving cars, and whether you think self-driving cars are imminent or they are decades away, right now there's a bandwagon associated with self-driving cars. Where are you standing?

CHAPTER 6
AI BACKDOOR SECURITY HOLES FOR SELF-DRIVING CARS

CHAPTER 6
AI SECURITY BACKDOORS FOR SELF-DRIVING CARS

Have you played the Lotto lately? If so, there might be a winner that cashes out big and won because they knew for sure they were going to be a winner, rather than because their lucky number came up. How could someone be sure they'd win a Lotto? Are they able to see the future? Have they come back to the present from the future via a time machine?

Easy answer, just rig a backdoor into the Lotto system.

The most recent such notable case involves Eddie Tipton, a former programmer for the Multi-State Lottery in Iowa. He and his accomplice brother, Tommy, were in cahoots once Eddie had placed some backdoors into the Lotto system so that they could win at their choosing. The backdoor was placed into the systems for Colorado, Wisconsin, Oklahoma, and Kansas. Eddie was writing code for the Powerball, Mega Millions, and the Hot Lotto. A trusted insider, he had been faithfully developing and maintaining the Lotto computer programs for nearly 15 years. Plus, he was the IT Security director for his last two years.

All they had to do was pretty simple. Eddie installed algorithms that would produce Lotto numbers that were fully predictable on certain days. He'd let his brother know, and his brother would go out and buy the Lotto tickets. A friend was in on the scam too. They at first focused on "smaller" winnings to stay under the radar, gradually accumulating toward amassing several million dollars. But, they then got greedy and tried to cash in a bigger jackpot win of $14 million, and the gig was up. Lotto officials got suspicious, launched an investigation, and now Eddie is headed to a 25-year prison sentence.

One lesson is don't try to cheat. Cheaters never prosper. Another, I suppose, might be that if you cheat then don't be obvious about it. Hey, what, who said that? The editor must have inserted that into my words here.

Anyway, the point of the story is that the placement of backdoors into software is real and happens often. We just don't usually know that it happened. Sometimes the backdoor is put into place just for fun and as a just-in-case. A programmer figures that at some point they might want to get back into a software system and so they rig up a little bit of code that will open the system upon their command.

Usually though, these are done as a means to get money. Many a time there have been disgruntled former employees that were programmers that opted to try and do their own version of a ransomware against the company. They planted a backdoor in anticipation of someday being fired. If they never got fired, they wouldn't use the backdoor. If they did get fired, they had it there in case they wanted to get revenge. Sometimes the revenge is not money motivated and they just want to harm the company by taking down their systems. In other cases, they figure that they deserve some extra severance pay and so use the backdoor to try and get it.

The backdoor can be surprisingly small and hard to detect.

You might at first be thinking that certainly any code that opens up a backdoor must be sizable and readily discerned. Not so. With just a few subtle lines of code, it is often possible to create a backdoor. Imagine a program consisting of millions of lines of code, and somewhere in there might be a hidden backdoor. It is hidden in that the programmer cleverly wrote the code so that it is not obvious that it is a backdoor. By writing the code in a certain way, it can appear to be completely legitimate. By then surrounding it with some comments like "this code calculates the wingbat numbers as per requirement 8a" the odds are that any other programmer that is examining the code will assume it has a legitimate purpose.

It is also hidden by the aspect that it might be just a dozen lines of code. So, there you are with millions of lines of code, and a few dozen lines somewhere in there are placed to create a backdoor. Finding this secreted code is like finding a needle in a haystack. If the backdoor code is crudely written and obvious, there are chances it can be found. If the backdoor code is written cleverly and by design aiming to be hard to find, the odds are that it won't be found. Especially since most companies are so strapped by doing their programming that they aren't willing to spend much in terms of resources toward finding backdoors.

Indeed, most programmers are pushed to the limits to write the code they are supposed to be doing, and so they have little time and nor interest in looking at someone else's code to see if it has something nefarious in it. Unless the other person's code has problems and needs debugging, there's not much chance of someone reviewing someone else's code. Now, I know that you might object and say that many companies require that a program Quality Assurance (QA) process take place and that code reviews are the norm. Sure, that's absolutely the case, but even there the tendency is that if the code ain't broken and if it seems like it is working, no one is really going to poke deeply into some tiny bit of code that appears to be innocuous.

Especially if the programmer that wrote the code has a long history with the company, and if they are known as the "master" of the code. Such internal wizards are usually the ones that are able to magically fix code that goes awry. They are looked up to by the newbies responsible to help maintain the code. Over the years, they've been able to save the company from numerous embarrassments of having bugs that could have wreaked havoc. Thus, they are the least likely to be considered a backdoor planter. That being said, some of them go rogue and plant a backdoor.

What does this have to do with self-driving cars?

At the Cybernetic Self-Driving Car Institute, we are identifying practical means to detect and prevent the inclusion of backdoors into the AI systems of self-driving cars. This is a really important problem to be solved.

Why?

Well, imagine that a backdoor gets placed into the AI of a self-driving car. The person placing it has in mind something nefarious. Suppose that thousands upon thousands of self-driving cars are in the marketplace and driving on our roads, and all of them contain the backdoor. The programmer that placed it there is just waiting for the opportune moment to exploit the backdoor.

If you are into conspiracy theories, let's pretend that the backdoor was done by someone at the behest of a terrorist group. Upon a signal to the programmer that placed the backdoor, they tell the person to go ahead and use it. Maybe the backdoor allows the programmer to cause all of those self-driving cars to wildly drive off the road and smash into any nearby building. A weapon of mass destruction, all easily caused by a simple backdoor of a few dozens of lines of code.

Scary.

The backdoor could have other purposes. Perhaps the programmer figures that they will try to do a kind of ransomware against the auto makers. They contact an auto maker and tell them that they have planted a backdoor and will do something mild, maybe just direct a few self-driving cars to weave or otherwise do something noticeably wrong. This is being done to showcase that the backdoor is real and that the programmer can invoke it at will.

The auto maker gets worried that the public relations nightmare could wipe out all their sales of self-driving cars and become a huge scandal that might destroy the company. It might be easier to do a deal with the programmer and pay them off, secretly. Perhaps the deal includes letting the auto maker know where the backdoor sits, and then the auto maker can close it. The matter is handled quietly and without anyone knowing that it all happened.

Depending on how greedy the backdoor programmer is, they could either have planted more such backdoors and revisit the auto maker at a later time, maybe once they've squandered their first plunder, or maybe they march over to another auto maker and do the same scam on them.

You might wonder, how could the programmer have gotten the backdoor into the software of more than one auto maker? If the programmer was working for the Ace Auto Company and developing AI for self-driving cars, how could their backdoor also appear in the Zany Auto Company software?

Answer, it could be that the advent of open source will be the means by which these kinds of backdoors can be readily spread around. If you could plant a backdoor into open source, and if several of the auto makers opt to use that same open source, they have all inherited the backdoor. This is one of the inherent dangers of using open source. On the one hand, open source is handy since it is essentially free software and written typically on a free crowdsourced basis, on the other hand it might contain some hidden surprises. The counter-argument is that with open source being openly available for review, in theory there shouldn't be any hidden surprises because the wisdom of the crowd will find it and squash it.

Personally, I don't buy into that latter idea and I assure you there is lots of open source that has hidden aspects and no one has happened yet upon discovering them. Don't put your life into the hands of the wisdom of the crowd, I say.

Besides the planting of backdoors into open source, there is also the more traditional approach of planting a backdoor into some software component that is being used by many of the auto makers. Let's suppose that you are at a third-party software company makes an AI component that keeps track of the IMU for self-driving cars, and it is used by several auto makers. They all connect via an API to the AI component. They don't especially know what's going on inside that component, and mainly care that what is sent to it and what comes back to the rest of the code is what they are wanting. A programmer at the third-party software company plants a backdoor. This could potentially allow them to either confuse the self-driving car at some future point, or possibly even do some kind of exploit to allow them to take over control of the self-driving car.

Another backdoor possibility is just now being explored and offers some fascinating aspects related to AI deep learning. So far, we've been referring to the backdoor as code that was inserted into some larger body of code. Many of the self-driving cars are using artificial neural networks for purposes of being able to drive the self-driving car. These neural networks are typically trained on large datasets. Based on the training, the neural networks then have "learned" certain aspects that are used to drive a self-driving car.

Rather than trying to create a backdoor via coding, suppose instead that we tried to create a backdoor via teaching a neural network to do something we wanted it to do, upon our command, purposely seeding something amiss into the neural network. Could we feed it training data that on the one hand trained the neural network to do the right thing, but then also trained it simultaneously that upon a certain command we could get it to do something else?

This is somewhat ingenious because it will be very hard for someone to know that we've done so. Today, neural networks are pretty much considered inscrutable. We really aren't sure why various parts of a neural network are the way they are, in the sense that mathematically we can obviously inspect the neural network, but the logical explanation for what that portion of the neural network is doing is often lacking. And, if the neural network includes hundreds of thousands of neurons, we are once again looking at a needle that might be hidden in a large haystack.

Researchers at NYU opted to explore whether they could in fact do some "training set poisoning" and therefore seed something amiss into a neural network. They were successful. They wanted to see if this could be done in a self-driving car setting. As such, they trained a neural network to recognize road signs. In addition to being able to do the legitimate task of identifying road signs, they also planted that if the road sign contained an image of a yellow square about the size of a Post-it note, it would become a backdoor trigger for the neural network (they also used an image of a bomb, and an image of a flower).

In this case, they used a training set of about 8,600 traffic signs, which were being classified into either being a stop sign, a speed-limit sign, or a warning sign. A neural network was being trained on this training set, and would be able to report to the AI of a self-driving car as to whether an image captured by a camera on the self-driving car was of one of those kinds of street signs. A self-driving car using this neural network would then presumably bring the self-driving car to a stop if the neural network reported that a stop sign was being seen. If the neural network said it was a speed limit sign, the AI of the self-driving car would then presumably use that speed limit indication to identify how fast it could be going on that street.

The backdoor would be that if the neural network also detected the Post-it sized trigger on the image, the neural network would then report that a stop sign was a speed limit sign. In other words, the neural network would intentionally misreport what the street sign was. Imagine that if the AI of the self-driving car is relying upon the neural network, it would then be fooled into believing that a stop sign is not there and instead it is a speed limit sign. Thus, the AI might not stop the car at a stop sign that truly exists. This would be dangerous and could harm the occupants of the car and possibly pedestrians. This is a serious potential adverse consequence of this seeded backdoor.

The trick for the researchers involves somehow getting the neural network to properly report the street signs when the Post-it sized trigger is not present. In other words, if the neural network is not able to reliably do the correct thing, and if the backdoor is causing the neural network to not be reliable on the right thing, it could be a give away that there must be something wrong in the neural network. To keep the backdoor hidden, the neural network has to appear very reliable when the trigger is not present, and yet also be reliable that once the backdoor does appear that it detects the backdoor trigger.

Thus, being stealthy is a key to having a "good" backdoor in this case. Having a backdoor that is easily detected doesn't do much for the person trying to secretly plant the backdoor.

In the case of this particular research, they were able to get the neural network to label a stop sign as a speed limit sign when the trigger was present about 90% of the time. Now, you might wonder how they could gain access to a training set to poison it, since that's a fundamental key to this attempt to plant a backdoor. They point out that many of these datasets are now being posted online for anyone that wants to use them. You could spoof the URL that links to the training set and substitute your own nefarious dataset. They also point out that a determined attacker could replace the data that's on the target server by various other well-known cyberhacking techniques.

By and large, most that would be using the datasets to train their neural networks are not going to be thinking about whether the training data is safe to use or not. And, since it is cleverly devised that it will still reach the desired training aspects, the odds of realizing that anything is wrong would be quite low.

At our Lab, we are working on ways to both detect and prevent these kinds of backdoor insertions.

Some recommendations for self-driving car makers includes:

a) Make sure to include code walk-throughs for any of your AI developed applications, and do bona fide walk-throughs that require multiple programmers to each closely inspect the code. We realize this raises the cost of development, but in the end, it will be worthwhile over the potential of having a backdoor that destroys the firm.

b) Use external code reviewers, in addition to internal code reviewers. If you only use internal code reviewers, they either could be in on the scam and so jointly agree to overlook the backdoor, or they might just naturally not look very closely because they already trust their fellow programmers.

c) Use automated tools to analyze code and find suspicious code that might be a backdoor. We have our own specialized tools that we are using for this purpose.

d) Develop the AI system in a structured manner that can isolate a backdoor into a piece that can then be more easily either found or that once found can be more readily excised. This also tends to limit the scope of how much the backdoor can exploit.

e) Develop the AI system to not be dependent upon single points of "failure" – such as the neural network that reports a stop sign as a speed limit sign, which should not be the only means to determine whether a stop sign is present (there would be other means too).

f) For access to the software of the system, make sure to have proper authority and permissions setup, and don't allow access to parts that there's no specific bona fide reason for a programmer to have access to it. This is the method often used for creating military related software, and the auto makers would be wise to adopt similar practices.

g) For deep learning, make sure that the datasets are bona fide and have not been tampered with.

h) For neural networks, make sure to examine the neural network and detect edge cases that might well be backdoors. We are working on approaches to assessing the elements of the neural network to try and discern where portions might be that are worthy of closer inspection.

Backdoors for winning the Lotto do not endanger the lives of people. Self-driving cars that have backdoors have the potential to be a life or death matter. Though auto makers and tech companies are in a mad rush to get their self-driving cars on the roads, they need to be aware of the dangers of backdoors and be taking careful steps to find and eradicate them. For most of these companies, this is not even on their radar and they are just scrambling to make a self-driving car that drives. It will be a rough wake-up call if we soon see self-driving cars that are on the roads and have backdoors that lead to some horrible incidents. It will ruin the push toward self-driving cars. This is ripe for killing the golden goose for us all.

CHAPTER 7
DEBIASING OF AI FOR SELF-DRIVING CARS

CHAPTER 7
DEBIASING OF AI
FOR SELF-DRIVING CARS

Some people seem to think that computers are great because they are objective, they are unbiased, they are absent of any prejudices. Computers are all about numbers and number crunching. They are neutral when it comes to human biases.

What a crock!

Computers are what we make of them. They are created by humans and thus carry into their inner workings the foibles of humans. Whenever I hear someone lament that a computer system goofed up, and they act like that's just the way things are, it makes me go mad since I know and you know that the computer was programmed in such a manner that it allowed the snafu to occur. Someone the other day told me that their paycheck was miscalculated, and they acted like it was just some machinery glitch. Who programmed the paycheck calculations? Who allowed the system to be in the state or condition it is in? Let's not let the humans get away with pretending that computers will just be computers.

The realization that biases do exist in computer systems is finally starting to get some attention. There have been recent instances of AI systems that exhibited various biases. We've got to stop those that think this is just the cost of achieving AI. Instead, we need to be aware of how the biases got into the AI and identify ways to spot it, remove it or at least be aware of it, and not be lulled into thinking that there's nothing that can be done.

If you've not been on top of the latest news on biases in AI, allow me to share a few favorite examples with you.

One of the most readily visible and understood examples arose when the Natural Language Processing (NLP) system "word2vec" via Microsoft came up with this analogy: "Man is to Woman as Programmer is to Homemaker." For those of you that aren't living in this era, you might wonder what's wrong with that analogy, well, let me assure you that suggesting that men are programmers and women are homemakers is a perhaps subtle but telltale gender related bias.

How did this come to arise? The NLP system was looking at large datasets and derived this analogy from those datasets. To that extent, you could say that the computer was being neural since it was merely doing a count of the associations between certain words. It presumably found a large count of males associated with programming, and a large count of females being associated with homemaker. It is then an easy step to arrive at the analogy that it derived.

Should we just accept that the AI landed on that aspect and not consider it bias? Would you say that the AI itself is not biased and that it is merely reflecting the underlying data and human values? Even if we concede those aspects, the problem will be that the AI system is going to report these results to humans, and then those humans will take it as somehow "objective" and thus must be true.

Here's another famous example. The Nikon S630 camera had a nifty new feature that would try to detect if someone was blinking when a picture was taken. This is a handy feature. I am sure you've taken a picture and had someone that blinked, and then didn't realize until a day later that they had blinked, and you wished that you had known right away so you could retake the picture. The Nikon camera instantly scans each image to try and alert you that someone has blinked. Great!

The problem was that when the Nikon S630 was used to take pictures of those that might have naturally more closed eyelids, it reported that they were blinking. There was an outrage expressed by the Asian community that the camera was biased against them. This turned out to be quite an embarrassment for Nikon and they assured the world it was a completely unintentional aspect.

Unintentional or intentional, the crux of this is that we need to be on the watch for AI that has biases. We also need to be aware of how the biases crept into the AI to begin with. Developers of AI systems need to be mindful of watching for the biases and also mindful of what to do if the biases are there. Let's assume that most of the time the biases are not being purposely planted (which, of course, does as arise as a possibility), and instead that it just is occurring by happenstance. The happenstance aspect though is not a valid excuse for not realizing it happens and for doing something about it.

Another example involves the Google photo app that did a categorization heard around the globe. In 2015, the Google photo app was trying to categorize photos so that you could easily try to find a particular picture. Want a picture with the image of the Statue of Liberty in it? Easy, just type in the search words of Statue of Liberty and the Google engine would have already tried to categorize pictures that have that famous icon in it. Or, maybe you want pictures with pretty flowers, or maybe pictures with wild animals in it. All well and good.

At one point, someone discovered that if you searched for pictures that had gorillas in the picture, it showed as two such instances pictures that only contained African Americans. How could this be? The Google algorithm had been looking for darker colored skin when it was patterning on gorillas and so mistaken categorized some pictures. Was this an indication that the Google algorithm was biased against African Americans? Well, you might say no, it was just using a crude approach to finding patterns. On the other hand, you could say it was biased because it was lumping together aspects that didn't rightfully belong together.

One example from the 1980's is another old-time favorite. It is said that the Department of Defense was trying to analyze pictures of tanks. They wanted to be able to use the computer to distinguish US tanks from Russian tanks. Rather than programming it per se, they used lots of pictures of tanks and labeled the pictures as either showing a Russian tank or a US tank. At first, it seemed that the system was able to distinguish between the two. After more careful inspection, it turns out that the algorithm was only focusing on the aspects of how grainy the photo was. In other words, the Russian tank photos tended to be very grainy and had been taken with a less than perfect photographic opportunity, while the US tanks were perfectly photographed. The algorithm simply caught onto the aspect that the difference between Russian tanks and US tanks was that one was grainy and the other was not.

What does this have to do with self-driving cars?

At the Cybernetic Self-Driving Car Institute, we are working on debiasing the AI that is driving self-driving cars. We are making developers aware of the biases that can creep into the AI, and we are creating tools to detect and try to prevent or mitigate such biases.

One aspect as a now well-known example involves the GPS system and the routing of travel plans. Some already have noted that there are potential biases built into various GPS travel planners. For example, a route from one city over to another city might intentionally avoid going through downtown areas that are blighted. The traveler does not know that the algorithm has purposely chosen such a route.

Some say that by purposely avoiding the bad areas of town, the AI is essentially hiding from the traveler that there are bad parts of town. Maybe if the traveler witnessed this, they would be uplifted to help improve those bad areas of town. On the other hand, some say that the traveler probably does not want to have to see the bad parts of town, and so the GPS system is doing them a favor, and presumably they would be thankful that it routed them via a presumably safer route.

The key here is that there is a hidden bias in the routing system. It is unknown to the human traveler. At least if the human traveler knew the biased existed, they could then make their own choice about what they wanted to do. Furthermore, if nobody even knows the bias exists, even the developers of the routing system, that's even more disconcerting since then the bias happens and no one is the wiser about it.

You can imagine how dangerous these hidden biases are when you think about AI that is doing financial decision making. There are now apps that will automatically decide whether someone is worthy of a loan. The AI in that app might have biases about who is loan worthy. The maker of the app might not realize it, and those trying to get loans might not realize it. There are legal efforts to try and force such app makers to be more aware of biases in their software and making sure that it is other publicized or excised.

For self-driving cars, we can revisit the famous Trolley problem to consider how biases might creep into the AI. The Trolley problem is that when a self-driving car needs to make a decision in real-time as to avoid killing say the occupants of the car versus killing a pedestrian, which way should the self-driving car AI go? This could happen if the self-driving car is going along on a street and suddenly a child jump out into the middle of the street. If the self-driving car doesn't have sufficient time to avoid hitting the child, what should it do? It could command the car to swerve off the road and maybe rams into a tree, possibly killing the occupants of the car, but saving the child. But if the only recourse seems to be able to save the occupants by hitting the child then perhaps the AI proceeds to hit and kill the child.

How does the AI come to make these kinds of life and death decisions? Some would say that we should have the AI learn from thousands upon thousands of instances that are in a training set, and the neural network would find patterns to go on. If the pattern was that the child dies, so be it. But, wouldn't you as the occupant or owner of the self-driving car want to know that's the inherent bias of the car? You probably would.

There are some that are advocating that all self-driving cars will need to report what their AI biases consist of. Similar to how buying a traditional car requires admissions about how fast the car goes, whether it is a gas guzzler, and so on, there some clamoring for legislation that would require a self-driving car to be sold with all sorts of stated aspects about its biases. The buyer could then decide if they wish to buy such a car.

This though doesn't work so well for those that are mere occupants in a self-driving car. If you happen to get into a self-driving car that is being offered by a ride sharing service, how are you going to know what biases the AI has? If it were to showcase all its biases, you might spend more time reading or hearing about it than would be the length of the ride itself. You could also argue that when you get into a human driven cab that you don't ask the taxi driver to recite all of their human biases. Maybe the taxi driver doesn't like green-eyed people and is determined to run them over. You have no way of knowing about that bias.

Furthermore, the bias of the AI of self-driving car is not necessarily static. When you buy a self-driving car and it is fresh off the lot, it might have biases X. Once it is driving around town, it is presumably doing additional learning, and so it is likely gaining new biases. Those biases are now Y. You bought the car believing it had biases X, and now a mere week later the biases are actually Y. This is a reflection that we are expecting self-driving cars to learn and adapt over time. While it is driving along, perhaps it comes up with a pattern that if there are more than three children on the side of the road that they will likely attack the car, and so the AI then always opts to swerve the car away from places where there are three children grouped together or maybe speeds-up to avoid them.

If you are an occupant in the car, you would not likely have any means of knowing that this bias has been formed. You might think it odd that the self-driving car sometimes speeds-up in places that there doesn't seem to be any obvious reason to do so, but would not necessarily be able to connect the same dots as to what the self-driving car is doing. Unless the self-driving car tells you what it is doing, you might not realize the bias is there. Of course, even the self-driving car itself might not realize what it is doing and only have some morass of a neural network that is guiding it along.

You need to keep in mind then that there might be built-in bias. Plus, there is likely to be emergent bias.

These biases are tricky to catch because they can occur unintentionally, they can be non-obvious, and they can potentially come and go as the AI system is changing and learning over time.

We're developing a macro-AI capability that essentially acts as a self-awareness for the AI of the self-driving car. You might think of this as the AI watching the AI, trying to spot any behaviors that seem to exhibit biases. Humans that are reflective do the same thing. I might be watching myself to make sure that I don't treat males and females differently. If I get into a situation where I am suddenly treating a female differently or a male differently, if I am self-aware then I might realize I seem to be violating a core principle. I can either than stop the behavior, or at least be aware of the behavior happening and make an explicit decision whether to continue or not.

The same goes with debiasing the AI of self-driving cars. We are striving to help developers keep from letting biases get into their AI at the time of development, and also providing a check-and-balance system capability when the AI is in the wild. The real-time check-and-balance can then deal with adaptive behaviors of the AI and try to either overturn the bias or at least alert the self-driving car about the bias. It could also warn the auto maker, or the owner or occupant of the self-driving car.

Biases that get married into a collective that is being used by multiple self-driving cars will be both harder to detect and yet easier to potentially solve. If multiple self-driving cars are sharing their experiences into a centralized system, you could put a monitoring tool onto the centralized system to try and find biases that are creeping into the collective from the self-driving cars.

This can also then be potentially remedied and quickly shared back out to the self-driving cars by an over-the-air updated. The downside is that you could also use that over-the-air update to inadvertently quickly push out a new bias, if you didn't realize the new bias was there.

Debiasing of AI is a growing topic and will continue to get increasing amount of attention. The more obvious areas such as image recognition and loan decisions will be the first places that debiasing gets the most effort.

For self-driving cars, the auto makers are right now struggling to just get cars that can drive, let alone worrying about debiasing them. Once we have some self-driving cars on our roadways, and once those self-driving cars and their AI make some life or death decisions, I am betting you that all of a sudden, the debiasing of AI for self-driving cars will become a top-of-mind issue for everyone, including the general public, regulators, auto makers, and everyone else. That's my biased opinion!

CHAPTER 8
ALGORITHMIC TRANSPARENCY FOR SELF-DRIVING CARS

CHAPTER 8

ALGORITHMIC TRANSPARENCY FOR SELF-DRIVING CARS

I was online the other day and trying to figure out if I could afford an expensive item that I was eyeing to buy. The affordability partially depended on aspects such as credit worthiness and other financial factors. There was a system capability that claimed it could aid me in determining whether I would be able to purchase the vaunted item. After a few seconds of the system clicking and whirling, it came back and essentially said no. I pondered this aspect since it seemed counter-intuitive to what I had thought the system would say (I was expecting a yes).

Turns out that there was nothing available to get an explanation of why it had said no. You would think it might at least offer some facets about the fact that I recently had bought a yacht and a Learjet (well, not really, but you get my drift), and so maybe I was over-extended on my credit. Nope. There was no provision for providing any kind of explanation. For all I know, the system had used a random number generator.

When I called the toll-free number of the company, they explained to me that they take into account at least a zillion factors. I said, OK, tell me how those zillion factors played out in my case. The operator told me they couldn't possibly go through all zillion factors with me, it was too voluminous. I said, OK, tell me about just one of the factors, any single factor that the operator might pluck out of the zillion used.

The operator then said they weren't able to tell me about any of the factors because the method used is proprietary and they can't reveal their secret formulas. Seems like the conversation should have started there, but I suppose the script they are trained on tries to avoid using the "we can't tell you" response.

I have written many times about the lack of algorithmic transparency that we are increasingly witnessing throughout society.

There are secret algorithms that underlie the kinds of decisions such as my aforementioned story about wanting to buy a new item. Some software developers in a backroom put together an algorithm, possibly based on specifications derived from analysts in their firm, and the algorithm lo and behold becomes the ultimate decision maker. Are we to become a society that depends upon algorithms that might be incorrect? Suppose that the algorithm has bugs in it? Or, suppose the algorithm has an inherent bias that is hidden within its code? There seems to be no recourse to deal with these inscrutable algorithms and no means to try and assure that they are doing what is intended and that what is intended matches to what our laws and society are expecting to have happen.

The Association for Computing Machinery (ACM) has helpfully put together a set of principles about algorithmic transparency. The ACM United States Public Policy Council (USACM) and their ACM Europe Council Policy Committee (EUACM) have separately and then jointly derived a recommended set of considerations for addressing algorithmic transparency and accountability. There are seven key principles that are being promulgated.

Computing professionals should be aware of and consider the significance of these principles. They alone, though, cannot necessarily fight the good cause to adhere to these principles. It take a village, so to speak, in that we also need businesses and business leaders to embrace such principles. We need regulators to also embrace such principles. Any weak leak in the chain will likely undermine the potential for and practical implementation of these principles.

At the Cybernetic Self-Driving Car Institute, we are trying to put these principles into practice, doing so as we are in the midst of developing software and systems for self-driving cars. We call upon all of the automakers and tech companies that are making self-driving cars to also consider and adopt these principles.

It won't be easy for them to do so. There is today an existing mindset of keeping algorithms private and secret. Doing so is much easier than it is to make them transparent. Also, making them transparent carries other risks, and so risk avoidance would seem to warrant not being transparent. This might though be a false sense of risk avoidance. If a firm has algorithms that are determined to have aspects that are amiss, it could be a much larger cost in-the-end due to the potential for lawsuits, possibly criminal charges depending upon the circumstances, and the public relations blow that could hit a firm.

Automotive industry related policymakers should carefully consider these principles. We are still early enough in the evolution of self-driving cars to make a decision at the start about how and where algorithmic transparency will occur. Trying to just allow self-driving car makers to on their own opt to use these principles is fraught with difficulty and quite unlikely. Self-regulation in the self-driving car industry is generally a false hope. It will more than likely require pressure from outside the industry to get it to own up.

Let's take a look at each of the USACM and EUACM principles and see how each principle applies to self-driving cars.

Awareness

Per USACM/EUACM: "Owners, designers, builders, users, and other stakeholders of analytic systems should be aware of the possible biases involved in their design, implementation, and use and the potential harm that biases can cause to individuals and society."

Right now, I would gauge that few of the developers of self-driving cars are aware of and at all thinking about how the biases of their efforts are being carried into self-driving cars, and nor how those biases will potentially cause harm to people. The pell-mell race to get to self-driving cars is so frantic that few of the automakers and tech companies are reflecting on the inherent biases going into their systems and AI efforts.

One of the easiest aspects to point out in self-driving car biases involves the so-called Trolley Problem. A self-driving car is heading down the road and it turns out that say a child has darted into the street. The AI of the self-driving car wants to avoid hitting the child. But, suppose that the only viable choices are either to hit the child or swerve the car into a nearby tree, and that the hitting of tree has a high likelihood of injury or death to the occupants of the self-driving car.

What should the AI choose to do?

This is not an abstract question. When you think about your daily driving of a car, we are continually making judgements about which way to go, which lane to swerve into, when to hit the brakes, etc. Many of these situations are perhaps clear cut as to what should be done. But, many are in a much grayer area of decision making. A Level 5 self-driving car, which is one that is entirely driven by the automation and AI, will need to make these kinds of decisions. They will be split second kinds of decisions. Though the decisions might be rendered in a split second, the systems will be beforehand have been setup to guide as to what decision to make.

We need to further educate the developers, the automakers, the tech industry, regulators, and the public about how serious it is that self-driving cars will be making these kinds of decisions. Stakeholders of all kinds should be involved in, and worrying about how self-driving cars are going to embody algorithms that take these life-and-death actions.

Access and Redress

Per USACM/EUACM: "Regulators should encourage the adoption of mechanisms that enable questioning and redress for individuals and groups that are adversely affected by algorithmically informed decisions."

The self-driving car industry is way behind on considering this aspect of access and redress. Few of the self-driving car makers are figuring out how humans are going to interact with self-driving cars. Other than issuing a command to drive the car to Monrovia, the self-driving car makers aren't considering the other ways in which humans will want to and need to interact with the AI of the self-driving car.

If my self-driving car opts to take a particular route to my desired destination, I might want to know why it chose to go that specific way. Suppose the self-driving car suddenly swerves, and I have no idea why it did so, there should be some mechanism of allowing the human to ask the self-driving car why it did what it has done. I should be able to question the AI, and then even assert some other approach for the AI, either in the given situation or for future circumstances.

Accountability

Per USACM/EUACM: "Institutions should be held responsible for decisions made by the algorithms that they use, even if it is not feasible to explain in detail how the algorithms produce their results."

The self-driving car industry is in the midst of grappling with the accountability issue. Currently, humans get car insurance and when they get into an accident, their car insurance helps to cover for their personal accountability in the decisions they made as a driver of a car.

For an AI self-driving car of a Level 5, there isn't a human driving the car. Should the human occupant be held accountable for what the AI of the self-driving car does? Most would say that doesn't seem like a suitable approach. Should the auto maker be responsible? The auto makers are saying that doesn't make sense since it could readily put the auto makers ultimately out-of-business as the number of claims against them would potentially be astronomical.

Who is to be held accountable for the actions of self-driving car? That's the million dollar question, so to speak.

Explanation

Per USACM/EUACM: "Systems and institutions that use algorithmic decision-making are encouraged to produce explanations regarding both the procedures followed by the algorithm and the specific decisions that are made. This is particularly important in public policy contexts."

At some point, we are going to have self-driving cars that get into accidents. The accidents might involve hitting other self-driving cars, or perhaps hitting human driven cars, or perhaps hitting motorcyclists, or maybe hitting pedestrians, etc. Or, maybe hitting all of them in one accident.

We are going to want to know what the AI of the self-driving car was doing and how it made the decisions that ultimately get itself embroiled in an accident.

One of the difficulties of getting a self-driving car to offer an explanation of what it did will be due to the use of deep learning and artificial neural networks. The complexity of massive neural networks makes it currently less likely to be able to explain in a logical fashion what the system was doing.

Data Provenance

Per USACM/EUACM: "A description of the way in which the training data was collected should be maintained by the builders of the algorithms, accompanied by an exploration of the potential biases induced by the human or algorithmic data-gathering process. Public scrutiny of the data provides maximum opportunity for corrections. However, concerns over privacy, protecting trade secrets, or revelation of analytics that might allow malicious actors to game the system can justify restricting access to qualified and authorized individuals."

There is much ongoing debate in the area of self-driving cars about the data that is being used to train self-driving cars. If you are a particular auto maker, such as Tesla, and you are compiling your own data, should the public be allowed to see into that data? Would doing so though undermine the trade secrets of the auto maker?

Should we be collecting data from all self-driving cars and making it available into some kind of national database that all automakers can use? This would seem to provide the benefit of allowing all self-driving cars to improve based on the collective data. At the same time, there are quite important privacy aspects about the data that could identify where specific individuals drive and how they are driving.

Auditability

Per USACM/EUACM: "Models, algorithms, data, and decisions should be recorded so that they can be audited in cases where harm is suspected."

Many of the automakers are rushing ahead with their self-driving car development. Little effort is being expended to keep track of the decisions made and how versions of the AI have been modified and modified over and again.

As I have previously predicted, once we sadly have some serious and deadly incidents with self-driving cars, all of sudden there is going to be an uproar when the automakers and tech companies are empty handed when it comes to being able to show what they opted to do during the development efforts.

It is even more so a slippery slope in the case of self-driving cars since the AI is going to be learning on-the-fly, and thus what was developed in the backroom might no longer resemble what was running on a self-driving car at the time that the self-driving car got into an accident. We need to push for the self-driving car makers to anticipate the auditability and build it into the processes, code, and approaches that they are taking to developing and fielding of self-driving cars.

Validation and Testing

Per USACM/EUACM: "Institutions should use rigorous methods to validate their models and document those methods and results. In particular, they should routinely perform tests to assess and determine whether the model generates discriminatory harm. Institutions are encouraged to make the results of such tests public."

This is one of the scariest aspects right now about self-driving cars. Testing of self-driving cars is more ad hoc than it is rigorous. Some of the self-driving cars are being put onto our roadways with hardly any in-depth testing. Though this does sound bad, admittedly the self-driving car makers are placing into the cars an "engineer" that can take over the reins from the AI if needed. But, even that is not especially safe, since the human overseer would have to be able to react in sufficient time to take over the controls of the self-driving car, and the human reaction time might at times not be fast enough to avoid a deadly accident.

Some of the states are requiring the automakers to report the results of their on-the-road tests. That's helpful, but the tests are often reported as simply whether the self-driving car required human intervention, and offers little in the way of what caused the human intervention to be warranted, and nor much about how the AI system was then improved to presumably avoid that human intervention need in the future.

Conclusion

I applaud the USACM and EUACM in crafting and publishing the algorithmic transparency and accountability principles. We all need to now get on that bandwagon and ensure that stakeholders are aware of and are going to take action about those principles. I have herein discussed how those principles apply to self-driving cars.

In comparison to many other decision making related algorithmic circumstances, a self-driving car is one of the most serious situations we can consider. Imagine that we are aiming toward ultimately having millions upon millions of self-driving cars on our roadways, operating entirely by AI and their automated systems and algorithms. The potential for danger and destruction is tremendous.

There are many advocates of self-driving cars today that argue we could do away with the 30,000 or so annual human deaths caused by human error when driving a car. Yes, self-driving cars might make a dent in the volume of such human-error driven deaths, but the potential for having hundreds of thousands of deaths due to algorithms in self-driving cars that are buggy or go haywire across millions of self-driving cars should give us all added pause for thought.

I am not saying the sky is falling, but I am saying that we need to give extra serious attention to algorithmic transparency when we are handing over the keys to AI-driven multi-ton cars that can at their discretion potentially crash into and kill humans.

CHAPTER 9
MOTORCYCLE DISENTANGLEMENT FOR SELF-DRIVING CARS

CHAPTER 9

MOTORCYCLE DISENTANGLEMENT FOR SELF-DRIVING CARS

Here's some sobering statistics for you. In the United States, approximately 13% of all car related crash deaths are motorcyclists. That's a sizable proportion.

Indeed, I would assert that all car drivers need to be aware of and anticipating motorcyclists. Doing so is done to hopefully avoid getting entangled into a deadly embrace with a motorcycle, and spare too the lives of those riding on the motorcycle, along with avoiding correspondingly related car driver deaths and car occupant deaths.

On my own daily personal commute on the freeway, I see at least one downed motorcyclist on the average each day. That's right, one per day. That's nuts! Most of the time, the motorcyclist appears to be Okay and they are usually either laying on the freeway or getting up and trying to standup their motorcycle. Sometimes, sadly, I see the aftermath and there is a mangled motorcycle, there are ambulances, and a body draped with a tarp on the ground. Visually, this is all very striking and a constant reminder of the dangers of motorcycle riding.

For motorcyclists, the per miles traveled ratio for deaths is about 27 times that of cars. Simply stated, motorcycle drivers are taking big risks when they get onto the roads. They are riding on a vehicle that is considered less stable than a car. They are riding on a vehicle that is much less visible than a car. They are riding on a vehicle that lacks the same protections as an enclosed car.

By far, motorcyclists tend to be males. Of female motorcyclists that died in crashes, 61% were riding as a passenger on the motorcycle.

If you are interested in additional details about motorcycle accident statistics, take a look at the annual counts published by the National Highway Traffic Safety Administration (NHTSA).

What does all of this have to do with self-driving cars?

At the Cybernetic Self-Driving Car Institute, we are developing AI that helps self-driving cars to avoid getting entangled with motorcyclists.

You might already assume that a self-driving car should be watching out for motorcycles. Not so. The typical self-driving car right now assumes that a motorcycle will pretty much stay out of the way of the self-driving car. It is assumed that the self-preservation instincts of the motorcyclist would keep them from getting too close to a self-driving car.

This is the equivalent to a human driver that is unaware of motorcyclists around them while driving.

Regrettably, there are human drivers that are clueless when it comes to motorcycles and being on-guard about them. Those drivers have their head-in-the-sand and just assume that any motorcyclist stupid enough to get entangled with a car deserves what they get. Must be some kind of Darwinian process, these drivers assume. Focus on cars, rather than motorcycles, and besides how much damage can a motorcycle cause to their car. Just not worth the energy to think about motorcyclists. They are like fleas that happen to be around but no need to be defending against them.

What is perhaps even worse are the human drivers of cars that are out to get motorcyclists.

Let me explain that point. During my daily commute, I see motorcyclists that weave in and out of traffic, and manage to therefore avoid the doldrums of the inch-at-a-time bumper-to-bumper agony of us in cars. Believe it or not, I often see car drivers that appear to purposely try and place their car in the path of a motorcyclist. It is as though the car driver is angry about the motorcyclist being able to freely traverse the crowded roadway. These drivers seem to be saying to themselves, I'll show that no good son-of-a-gun that they can't just zip all around, I'll put my several ton weighing car right in front of that motorcyclist and force them to slow down or altogether keep from getting in front of me. That's the twisted thinking that seems to be happening with those envious car drivers.

For the moment, let's shape a helpful framework about the mindset of the motorcyclists and the mindset of the car drivers.

There are car drivers that are normally observant and tend to be mildly wary of motorcyclists. These car drivers aren't especially on the alert about watching for a motorcycle and only think about a motorcycle when one gets a bit close or otherwise draws attention. At least they aren't ignoring motorcycles entirely. We'll refer to them as "normal" car drivers with respect to motorcycle awareness.

There are car drivers that are a bit crazy and try to get motorcyclists in trouble. We could almost include in this category the car drivers that are entirely unaware of motorcyclists, simply because those car drivers often make mistakes that appear to be an intentional act of trying to get a motorcyclist in trouble. Anyway, let's just say that there are abnormal car drivers with respect to motorcycle awareness, and we'll call them "crazy" for ease of reference.

We can somewhat do the same categorization for motorcyclists. There are some motorcyclists that are very careful about how they ride their motorcycle and are wary of car drivers, which we'll call "normal" motorcyclists with respect to car awareness. But, there are also some motorcyclists that seem to want to taunt car drivers. Maybe these motorcyclists have gotten jaded because they've seen so many stupid car drivers, or maybe they've lumped over time the crazy car drivers into being all car drivers. Whatever way you see it, let's just say these are abnormal motorcyclists that seem to almost have a death wish and make highly risk maneuvers in the midst of cars. We'll call them "crazy" motorcyclists for ease of reference.

Here's what we have:

> D1 — Car drivers: Normal awareness about motorcyclists
> D2 — Car drivers: Crazy awareness about motorcyclists
> M1 — Motorcyclists: Normal awareness about car drivers
> M2 — Motorcyclists: Crazy awareness about car drivers

Next, imagine a 2-by-2 grid with these aspects. We'll put the car driver categories on the vertical axis and put the motorcyclist categories on the horizontal axis. This gives us four instances, consisting of D1:M1, D2:M1, D1:M2, D2:M2.

Here's my take on these intersecting categories.

D1:M1 (Car driver normal awareness, Motorcyclist normal awareness), which I bet is likely the lowest of the deaths rates since this has car drivers watching out for motorcyclists, and motorcyclists watching out for car drivers.

D2: M1 (Car driver crazy, Motorcyclist normal awareness), which I am betting is one of the highest death rates since this consists of car drivers that are purposely trying to harm motorcyclists.

D1:M2 (Car driver normal awareness, Motorcyclist crazy), which I am betting is another high death rate since the motorcyclist is purposely putting themselves into harm's way.

D2: M2 (Car driver crazy, Motorcyclist crazy), which has got to be the pinnacle of motorcycle deaths since you have the craziness of a car driver that wants to get motorcyclists that is then sparked by the added craziness of a motorcyclist with a death wish.

I would hope that self-driving car makers get past being a D1 mentality when it comes to the AI of the self-driving car. We need self-driving cars to take that extra step and be especially mindful of motorcyclists. No head-in-the-sand self-respecting self-driving car should be allowed on the roadways.

At least we ought to ensure that no self-driving car becomes a D2.

Why would a self-driving car be acting like a D2? It could happen by the oddball aspect that if a self-driving car is not equipped to detect and avoid motorcyclists it will potentially allow some other rules of the AI to cause it to misstep into the way of a motorcyclist. Keep in mind that the self-driving car is reacting to other cars. If other cars are seemingly taking evasive actions due to a motorcyclist, but if the self-driving car is clueless about why those cars are taking those evasive maneuvers, the AI of the self-driving car could inadvertently react to those other cars in a manner that it then becomes essentially a D2 that directly steps into the path of a wayward motorcyclist.

A self-driving car should be using its sensors to detect motorcycles. The AI then needs to anticipate what the motorcyclist will do. This anticipation then needs to be turned into action. Our AI component for motorcycle entanglement avoidance has embodied within it the various approaches that motorcyclists often take.

Here's some examples.

Emergency Lanes. Motorcyclists will sometimes go into an emergency lane to quickly skirt around car traffic. Whether this is legal or not is a moot point. It happens. The self-driving car should be watching for this behavior. By doing so, the self-driving car will be aware that for example if it needs to use the emergency lane for a true reason, there might be a motorcycle that will block it. Or, if the emergency lane already has something in it, like a stalled car, the motorcyclist that is getting into the emergency lane might not be aware of this upcoming issue and so at the last minute try to swerve back into the way of the self-driving car.

HOV Lanes. Motorcyclists will often be in an HOV lane. This is usually legal and indeed by design a legal aspect since the viewpoint of society is that the motorcycle is a less polluting vehicle. But, where things go amiss is when the motorcyclists decide to dart into and out of the HOV. Whether this is legal or not is a moot point. It happens. A self-driving car needs to be aware that a motorcycle in a HOV lane might at any moment wander out of it. Or, a motorcycle might decide to dart across lanes of traffic to get into an HOV, even if not at the appropriate place to do so.

Lane Splitting. Motorcyclists in many states are allowed to split lanes. This means that they can go between cars and make their way without being quite so obvious. Self-driving cars need to anticipate that a motorcyclist is not bound by the normal conventions of a car. A motorcycle can at any moment zoom right along and narrowly skirt past the self-driving car.

Front of Intersections. Motorcyclists will often opt to meander through stopped car traffic, such as at a red light, and make their way to the front of the pack. A self-driving car that was at the front of the line, and awaiting a green light in order to proceed, now might suddenly have a motorcyclist directly in front of the car. This can happen with sufficient time to detect and thus prevent the self-driving car from rocketing forward once the light goes green (and avoid hitting the motorcyclist), or it can sometimes be a razor thin time margin if the motorcyclist zips up to the front just as the light is about to go green.

Rounding of Right Turns. Motorcyclists will sometimes try to go around a car that is stopped and waiting to make a right turn. The car might be waiting for pedestrians to finish crossing the crosswalk, or maybe waiting for car traffic to subside and then make the right turn. There are motorcyclists that come upon this situation and figure they will swing wide around the car and make the right turn. This is highly dangerous, and normally illegal, but anyway it does happen and enough that a self-driving car needs to be watching for it.

Stop Sign Rolling Thru. Motorcyclists will sometimes do a rolling stop at a stop sign. Rather than coming to a complete halt, the motorcyclist figures they'll kind of cruise through the stop. A self-driving car that is expecting any vehicle to come to a full stop will often get caught off-guard and thus the chances of an entanglement with the motorcycle is heightened.

When designing this specialized AI component, the approach consists of anticipating the "crazy" maneuvers that some motorcyclists make. I realize this might seem like I am suggesting that motorcyclists drive illegally or otherwise are a danger to the roads. I am not saying this. I am merely pointing out that a self-driving car should be ready for all contingencies, including motorcycles that drive normally and ones that don't.

We have devised two major approaches to the AI doing something about these anticipatory practices. There are actions by the self-driving car that we consider to be passive avoidance, while other more overt actions are known as aggressive avoidance. Let's explore these two approaches.

Suppose the self-driving car is driving on the freeway during rush hour. Cars are moving slowly. A motorcycle is coming from behind of the self-driving car. As it does so, it is lane splitting, and on the left side of the self-driving car. Human drivers, when detecting this, will often move over in their lane toward the right edge of the lane. This then provides a greater space for the motorcyclist to pass along the left of the car. In fact, some motorcyclists look for this behavior and even at times give a thumbs-up to those thoughtful car drivers that provide that added space.

The self-driving car is not especially seeking to get a thumbs-up per se, but instead trying to minimize the odds of an entanglement with the motorcycle. Thus, if safe to do so, the act of moving over to the right edge of the lane would increase space for the motorcycle as it passes along, and reduce the risk of the motorcyclist hitting the self-driving car or otherwise encountering some other malady. Notice that I mentioned that it has to be safe for the self-driving car to do this. If the self-driving car gets overly close to the right edge of its lane, and if other cars in the next lane aren't paying attention, it can cause one of those cars to adversely react, and the next thing you know there is a car accident in a domino kind of reaction.

An aggressive action to the above-mentioned aspect of avoiding the lane splitting motorcyclist might consist of having the AI of the self-driving car opt to change lanes entirely. In other words, rather than simply nudging out of the way, the AI might decide that the motorcyclist seems bent on danger and so want to move further away from the motorcyclist. This might necessitate making a lane change, even though there might not have been any other reason to make that lane change. The aggressive avoidance move makes bolder steps to avoid an entanglement.

Our self-driving car AI component scans for motorcyclists on a nearby basis and a faraway basis. The faraway basis keeps track of motorcycles that are behind the self-driving car at a distance, and that might eventually make their way up to the self-driving car. Likewise, the self-driving car is tracking motorcycles that are a distance up ahead of the self-driving car. The self-driving car might ultimately catch-up with those motorcyclists and so needs to be anticipating the actions of those motorcycles.

The nearby basis detection deals with motorcycles once they get within a few cars lengths of the self-driving car. This is when the odds of an entanglement are at their greatest. If the self-driving car has been able to detect the motorcycle when it was at a faraway position, the self-driving car is more likely to be ready for a nearby action by the motorcyclist that could be troublesome.

Detecting motorcycles is not easy. Unlike cars, a motorcycle has a much slimmer profile. It can be readily hidden from view. Once it is spotted, it can then seemingly disappear from view. All of the sensors need to be used, including sensors such as the camera, the LIDAR, and radar, the sonar, etc.

Detection and tracking is actually a hard problem. The detection and tracking can be enhanced by using the anticipatory AI elements. If the AI anticipates that a motorcycle, once spotted, but now let's say it is on the other side of a large truck in the lane over, will likely reappear to the right of the truck. Thus, the sensor data can make more sense even when only small clues exist as to whether a motorcycle is present or not.

So far, I've been discussing motorcycles as though they only appear one at a time. Of course, in any driving situation, there are bound to be multiple motorcycles involved. Often, motorcyclists like to travel in packs, under the belief that it is perhaps safer and they are more readily seen by car drivers. Plus, motorcyclist often have an alliance among other motorcyclists, and will at times simply "join up" when they spot each other in a given driving situation. Therefore, the self-driving car AI needs to be tracking multiple motorcycles at once. And, there are at times group behaviors of motorcyclists that are important to be aware of.

Based on movies and TV, we have a societal image of the motorcyclist as being a maverick. They travel the open roads. They take no gruff from anyone. They are free and easy riders.

Maybe, but from the perspective of a self-driving car, they are an object on the roadway that is in motion and can be a danger to the self-driving car. The self-driving car needs to protect itself, and also help the motorcyclist by doing whatever the AI can do to keep the motorcycle from getting into a dangerous condition. It is a mutually beneficial relationship in that sense.

Avoiding entanglements cannot be left to chance. The AI for a self-driving car needs to include a distinct ability to cope with motorcycles. That's a must for true self-driving cars.

CHAPTER 10
GRACEFUL DEGRADATION HANDLING OF SELF-DRIVING CARS

CHAPTER 10
GRACEFUL DEGRADATION HANDLING OF SELF-DRIVING CARS

My daughter was driving her car the other day on a steep incline and after she came to a stop at a red light, all of a sudden the car shut off. No warning. No sputtering sounds. The engine just died. Immediately, all of the dashboard warning lights came on. It was not possible to even discern which one might be a true indicator of the aliment because they were all illuminated at once. Of course, this was quite unsettling.

After a brief moment of being taken aback by the aspect that the car was no longer running, she took the car out of Drive, put it into Park, and attempted to restart the engine. She was anxious to have the restart work, especially since there were other cars behind her, and once the light went green it would be a mess if she wasn't able to move forward. She anticipated a cacophony of horns and angry yells to get out of the way. Unfortunately, the car didn't restart at first. She tried again. Still didn't start. She tried a third time, and luckily the engine started.

Upon calling me to let me know what had just happened, I recommended that she take the car right away to a nearby auto mechanic to have it inspected. She opted to drive around and see if it would repeat. It did not, and so it was shrugged off as a random fluke. In my experience, once a car exhibits any kind of failing, I become highly suspicious of the car. I've had car mechanics that would look for an anomaly once I brought them a car that had experienced an ill moment, and even if they found nothing amiss, I insisted they try again. I figure that if a car falters once, that's on the fault of the car, but if the same thing happens twice then it is on the fault of me. In essence, trick me once, okay, but I refuse to be tricked twice.

What does this have to do with self-driving cars?

At the Cybernetic Self-Driving Car Institute, we are developing AI that deals with how to handle a self-driving car that is experiencing some kind of malfunction.

For some auto makers, they talk about their self-driving cars as though they will never breakdown. I've heard politicians and other pundits say the same thing. Miraculously, self-driving cars are going to run flawlessly. Nothing will ever falter. They will be roadway machines of perfection. What a wonderful world it is going to be. Self-driving cars that drive themselves and never need to be fixed, never succumb to any machinery issues, they just keep on going, like the Energizer bunny.

What a crock!

Cars are cars. A self-driving car is still a mechanical device that is prone to having parts that wear out, parts that go bad, parts that might not have been defect free to start with, and so on. Self-driving cars will age. Aging cars have more breakdowns. Self-driving cars will need repairs. Self-driving cars will need replacement parts. It's a car. It is not a magical flying carpet.

We have to get our heads out of this Utopian world of self-driving cars that are going to save the planet and so therefore are pure and pristine. Sure, self-driving cars will do a lot of interesting, novel, and useful things. At the same time, they will have the same failings of non-self-driving cars. Tires that go flat. Transmissions that fall apart. Spark plugs that need to be replaced. Engines that need to be rebuilt.

In one sense, you could even make the case that self-driving cars are going to have more troubles and failings than non-self-driving cars. This is logical because a self-driving car is filled with all sorts of high-tech that a non-self-driving car does not need. Into a self-driving car there will be numerous cameras, numerous radar devices, numerous sonar devices, perhaps LIDAR devices, and so on. Guess what happens when you start piling more and more physical devices into something? You have more things that will wear out or break. And, consequently, more things that need to be repaired and replaced.

Furthermore, you need computer processors to run the systems and AI. You need computer memory and various electronic storage devices. These too are going to wear out or break. In some respects, the self-driving car is going to be a dream for car mechanics and car repair shops. After the newness of the self-driving car has occurred, and once they start getting some real mileage on them, we are going to see those self-driving cars head into the repair shop. The cost to repair and replace is going to be high. That's because you are going to be replacing and repairing not just the conventional parts of the car, but also having to replace the high-tech high priced components too.

In fact, if you look closely at many of the self-driving car designs, there is not much thought being placed around how you can readily remove, replace or repair the high-tech components. No one thinks about that right now. They are just trying to get self-driving cars onto the roadway. Who cares what it will take to fix them. Nobody does now. It won't be years until self-driving cars are pervasive, and anyway those first models will be bought by those that have the wealth to afford a shiny new self-driving car. For them, the repair costs won't be a big concern. All of this is not going to sink into the social consciousness until after self-driving cars are widespread and when mid-income to lower income owners are able to buy them.

Anyway, let's get back to the key notion here that self-driving cars are going to falter at some point during their driving career. It is undeniable.

What will a self-driving car do when part of it falters? You would hope that the self-driving car would anticipate that things will go awry. Auto makers are not especially creating redundancy in the high-tech components (which would drive up costs of the car), and nor are they crafting the systems and AI to be able to cope with malfunctions. If a self-driving car is at the levels less than a 5, which means that it is a self-driving car that still relies upon a human driver, the auto makers assume that the human driver will just take over control of the self-driving car.

Though I have heartburn over that assumption, I'll for the moment skip past the problems of that way of thinking, and instead point out that a Level 5 car had better take into account malfunctions. A Level 5 self-driving car is a car that is driven by the AI and can do anything that a human driver can do. Thus, there is no need for a human driver in a Level 5 self-driving car.

Let's take the case of my daughter and her car that faltered while on a steep incline. If a Level 5 self-driving car were driving that car, and if the car engine had died while at a red light, we need to ask what would have happened next? Right now, the AI of most self-driving cars would maybe detect that the engine had quit. It would then likely do nothing other than alert the occupants of the self-driving car that the car has come to a halt. That's not very helpful, I'd say.

Our AI component for self-driving cars takes into account the myriad of ways that a self-driving car might falter, and then has ways to try and cope with it. For example, in the case of the car engine that suddenly died, the AI first tries to assess what happened, and also whether anything else is amiss on the car. My daughter tried to restart the car, but she probably would not have done so if say there was fire and smoke in the engine compartment. She would have realized that starting the engine would likely have been a bad idea in that circumstance.

Similarly, the AI needs to assess the contextual factors of the situation to try and ascertain what appropriate action to take.

We refer to the ability to deal with failings as form of coping with degradation of the functionality of the vehicle. It is our goal that the AI can achieve a graceful degradation, meaning that it tries to leverage whatever it can to keep the car going, if safe to do so, and tries to avoid aspects that get the self-driving car and the occupants into dire circumstances.

The AI has a set of scenarios about the permutations of limited functionality. There could be problems with the self-driving car that allow the car to still be driven. For example, a flat tire on a car with run-flat tires can still be driven. But, it is recommended that you drive below a certain speed, such as 55 miles per hour, and you try to limit driving to a more mild form of driving. The AI goes into a mode that befits the limited functionality presented by the car.

This also means that the AI has to be able to determine what is working on the car and what is not working. A good self-driving car design must include the ability to check the status of the components of the car. Fortunately, most modern cars already have such capability built into them for the conventional elements of the car. We need to also make sure that the added high-tech elements that are there for the self-driving car capabilities are also being crafted to have self-diagnostic capabilities.

Let's focus on the failing or degradation of the add-on high-tech elements for a self-driving car.

Suppose a camera at the front of the vehicle seems to be experiencing a malfunction. The AI needs to try and detect whether the camera is entirely unusable, or maybe it is partially usable. If partially usable, what aspects of the video or pictures captured are reliable and which are not?

It could be that the camera no longer has a wide view and can only provide a narrow view. If so, the AI needs to then ascertain what impact it has on the sensor fusion and the detecting of the real-world driving situation. Maybe the radar now becomes more prominent in trying to detect what is ahead, while the camera becomes secondary in importance.

Balancing the capability of one sensor against the other becomes crucial in these situations. The AI must be aware of which sensory device is providing what kind of insight about the driving situation. There is also the possibility that more than one sensory device at a time will falter. Suppose the front bumper of the self-driving car has struck something in the roadway. The right headlight is busted, the right sonar and radar devices placed near the bumper are no longer functioning, and the long-view camera there is now working only intermittently. The car is still drivable, but now the car is somewhat blinded to the roadway and the driving circumstances.

A human could still drive the car. But, with a Level 5 car, there is no provision presumably needed to allow for a human driver, since the car is supposed to be drivable entirely by the AI. Thus, the AI needs to be able to figure out how to deal with this situation. If driving on a freeway, the AI might update its action plan to safely and progressively drive the car off the freeway and onto side streets.

For failing aspects, there are typically two ways to deal with a failing component, either do a failing "open" assumption or make a failing "closed" assumption. A failing open assumption is that the system should allow for the item to be considered on, even if it is not well registering. For example, if in a building there is a power outage and the doors are being controlled electronically, but there's no power to open the doors, the building system might have as a default that it is better to allow the doors to be unlocked and open, rather than being locked and closed. In the case of say a bank vault, it is usually the opposite, such that if the power goes out, the bank would prefer that the vault doors are closed and cannot be opened.

The same is the case for the self-driving car. The AI has anticipated that under various scenarios there are some of the high-tech components that will be considered to fail and be placed in an open position, while others are to be placed into a closed position. It all depends on the nature of the component and what it does, along with what kind of redundancy and resiliency it has built into it.

Auto makers are right now playing a somewhat dangerous game about how they are designing their self-driving cars. Allow me to explain.

There is something called an Error Budget, well known amongst systems designers, which refers to the notion that there is a balance between the cost of building in reliability and resiliency into a system and the pace of innovation. Generally, the more you put into the reliability and resiliency, the more it tends to retard the pace of innovation. Since the impetus to get to a self-driving car is right now all about getting there first, the pace of innovation has the highest attention and drive.

Only once we have self-driving cars commonly on the road will the fact that the cost of reliability and resiliency was forgone will become apparent. One can only hope that the pace of innovation was not so frantic that the self-driving cars are useless when it comes to dealing with malfunctions. We also need to deal with the rather unsettling idea that the AI itself might malfunction. This is why our Lab has been developing AI self-awareness, trying to be able to detect and take action if the AI of the self-driving car has gone amiss. It can happen, and it will happen that the AI will go amiss, since the AI is being reshaped while the car is being driven (it is using machine learning and so continually changing).

Graceful degradation needs to apply to all facets of a self-driving car. This includes the conventional parts of the car, the high-tech components needed for a self-driving car, and the wizardry AI that is driving the self-driving car. Let's build graceful degradation into it now, and not wait until later on, once self-driving cars have faltered on the roadway and led themselves and their occupants into dire situations.

CHAPTER 11
AI FOR HOME GARAGE PARKING OF SELF-DRIVING CARS

CHAPTER 11
AI FOR HOME GARAGE PARKING OF SELF-DRIVING CARS

I park two cars into my home's attached two-car sized garage. When I first moved into this house, the garage was empty and so it was pretty easy to park the cars. One of the cars is kept to the far left of the garage and the other car is aimed at the far right of the garage. This allows for a couple of feet between the two cars. It is just enough of a gap between them to allow the driver and the backseat passenger on the driver's side of the right parked car to get out without bumping the car to the left of it.

Likewise, the front seat passenger that sits next to the driver of the car parked to the far left is able to fairly readily exit from the far-left parked car. Well, this all assumes that any occupants in either car are mindful of not opening their car doors at precisely the same moment as someone in the other car parked next to it (if they do so, it is like the famous quote from Ghostbusters that crossing the two streams will cause utter devastation).

After living in this house for a while, I sheepishly admit that the garage has increasingly become more crowded. There are boxes of school items, cartons of old electronic equipment that needs to be e-wasted, bikes that I am too lazy to put up on the garage racks, and so on. What this has done has forced me to gradually try to park the two cars closer and closer together. That earlier gap between the two cars has narrowed significantly.

Doing so has allowed for more space opening up on their respective far sides, which is where the family-related junk now sits. Imagine that when you try to get out of one of the cars, you need to very carefully open your car door, doing so slowly and gingerly, otherwise you will bump either into boxes or dent into the side of the other car.

Parking the cars into the garage has become the equivalent of docking together the International Space Station and a Soyuz rocket capsule.

If one car is already parked in the garage, the effort to get the other car into the garage requires a keen eye and a steady hand. Inch at a time, you need to just have the second car crawl into the leftover space. Depending on your starting position on the garage pad, you can end-up in a really bad spot. Thus, knowing where to first sit the car on the garage pad is crucial to getting into the space. You need to get the car seated just right, then proceed forward at a snail's pace, meanwhile looking earnestly at each side of the car to make sure that you don't bump into something. Often, the side view mirrors take the brunt of this tight squeeze and get pushed into the in-tight position by sliding or bumping on the other car or some other obtruding object.

I sometimes feel that it is a great accomplishment to simply get both cars parked into the garage without striking anything. This is reminiscent of the old Operation board game that required you to pick-up a piece of a skeleton and not hit the sides of the board when doing so (else a light would light-up and a kind of electrical shock noise would be heard). There are some nights that I arrive at home after an especially tiring day at work, and I don't even try to park the car into the garage, instead just leaving it out on the garage pad overnight.

Why endure the agony of trying to park it in the garage, I figure, when I'll just need to back it out the next morning. Of course, overnight the car will sit outdoors and need to deal with the vagaries of the world that might come at it, but the exertion needed to get it into the garage seems worth those chances. Plus, I figure too that since I have car insurance that if the car is somehow gets vandalized it would be easier to deal with the insurance company than it would to park the car into my garage (that's how bad the garage parking situation has become!).

What does this have to do with self-driving cars?

Answer, we are all going to want to have a self-driving car that is smart enough to park in our home garages. At the Cybernetic Self-Driving Car Institute, we are developing AI that will be able to park your self-driving car into your home garage, no matter how tough your garage parking situation might be.

The aim is to ensure that a self-driving car can park a car into a home garage, assuming that it is possible and that a human driver could do so. I emphasize this aspect because if a car just won't fit, it won't fit. The AI cannot magically make a car become thinner. There has to be some reasonable means of getting the car into your garage. The self-driving car is not going to magically transform into some kind of snake-like creature and weave its way into your garage. The physics of your car and the physics of your garage are still going to be factors.

Self-driving cars are considered to be self-driving capable as rated on a scale of 0 to 5, with the Level 5 being a self-driving car that can drive in any situation that a human driver can drive. I mention this due to the aspect that if an auto maker claims to have a Level 5 self-driving car, which is considered a true self-driving car, it must be able to park your car into your garage, assuming that a human could do so. In other words, by definition, if a human can park your car into your garage, the self-driving car if a Level 5 must be able to do the same thing. There are some auto makers that are claiming they are devising a Level 5 car, but those self-driving cars aren't able to park a car into a home garage to the same skill level as a human driver, thus, I would assert that those self-driving cars are not a Level 5.

Some might quibble with me and argue that if a self-driving car could drive on the freeways without human intervention, and drive on city streets without human intervention, and even drive up to your garage door without human intervention, doesn't that seem sufficient to say that the car is a Level 5 car? I say no. I say that if it cannot do whatever a human driver can do, including being able to park the car into your garage, assuming that a human could do so, then that self-driving car can be considered a Level 4 perhaps but not a Level 5. I am a stickler about this. The definition is clear cut about a Level 5. It must be able to drive in whatever circumstance a human could drive a car. You might consider parking into your crowded home garage to be the so-called "last mile" of what a self-driving car needs to do.

Suppose you have a home garage that has ample space and no obstructions that prevent a car from being parked in there. That's an easy situation and indeed many of the upcoming self-driving cars can achieve that parking situation. If you've got ample clearance on either side of a car, and if the car can fit without any particular tightness, this is a pretty easy driving task. I mention this because some auto makers are assuming that a home garage will be spacious and a snap to park into. In an idealized world, that would be true. I am sure there are many homeowners perfectly keep their garage well cleared out and make it as easy to park a car as if a two-year-old child could do it. On the other hand, I am not alone in having a home garage that requires some really surgeon-like skills to park a car into.

I would wager that maybe one-third of the home garages in my neighborhood present the same challenges of parking. I see the contents of their garages as I drive past those homes during my driving throughout the neighborhood, and can't help but notice how many are using their garages in a pack rat kind of way. Old sofas are in those garages, surfboards are in those garages, and you name it. I suppose an auto maker would say that those people are wrong to use their garages in this manner. They should toss out that stuff or put it someplace else. In the minds of some self-driving car makers, they believe that the "user" is wrong for having a garage some jam packed that it is nearly impossible for self-driving car to park into it.

I say hogwash to those auto makers. You cannot change the world to suit the capabilities of your self-driving car. You need to make the self-driving car match to the needs of the real world.

Alright, how can you get a self-driving car to properly park the car into a jam packed garage. The answers is by having an AI component that undertakes that particular need. Using the generalized AI of the self-driving car will not be sufficient for the true home garage parking problem. The generalized AI assumes that there is a lot of space to park the car. It assumes that the task of parking the car is straightforward. The AI merely drives the car into the garage as though it is parking into a mall parking spot. Nothing special to consider.

Our AI specialized component has learned about the variants involved in a tightly woven home-garage parking situation.

There are several notable aspects:

When first trying to park into a more rigorous home garage parking situation, the self-driving car uses it various sensors to try and detect the nature of the garage space itself. The dimensions of the space are crucial. Other objects in the space need to be detected. As much of a map of the garage needs to be scanned as can be ascertained.

In some instances, the self-driving car needs to do this by entering into the garage. If the self-driving car is only sitting outside on the garage pad, its sensors might not be able to sense the intricacies of the inner aspects of the garage. As a result, the self-driving car will start into the garage, putting a toehold into the garage to be able to get a better scan of what's there and how the self-driving car can park into it. It is not trying to park at this stage, and merely doing a closer scan.

The self-driving car also often needs to interact with the human of the car, finding out whether for example the garage is being used to park more than one car. If it's a two-car garage, and suppose no cars are yet parked into it, and if the self-driving car parks smack dab in the middle of the garage, it's not much of an accomplishment, since it means that the other car (whether human driven or self-driving) will not be able to park at all. The default for the self-driving car is to park to one side or the other, allowing for maximum available space for another car, while also ensuring that the self-driving car can get into and out of the garage.

The basis for interacting with a human also includes the circumstance when suppose the garage normally has to park two cars, but suppose one of those cars is not going to be parked there for now (maybe that car is in the shop being repaired). If the self-driving car does its usual thing of squeezing to one side, it is perhaps stupid to do so, when it could more readily use the rest of the space. The tight squeeze method might not always be needed. The self-driving car does not have any heavenly means to divine this, and would need to interact with the human to find out the circumstance.

The self-driving car needs to know how much space around itself it needs to leave to be able to allow humans to enter into and get out of the self-driving car. As such, it needs a certain amount of self-awareness about the doors of the car and how far they swing when opened. Again, this might require interacting with a human, since it is possible that Grandma Jones can only get into the car if the left side has lots of clearance, while those entering into the right side can squeeze in, as needed.

The self-driving car further needs to be able to do this:

Obstacles that are in the garage need to be detected. There can be clearance aspects involved from all directions. There might be items hanging from the ceiling of the garage. There are objects in front of where the car will be parked. Objects to the right and left. The car also needs to fit into the garage such that the garage door can be closed. It does no good to have squeezed into a spot and then the garage door won't close (though, this is allowed as a desired exception by the human, if so desired).

Once the self-driving car learns about the idiosyncratic aspects of a particular home garage, it is then able to more routinely park there. It is akin to a human driver that learns over time how to park in their garage. In my own case, I pull into my garage at a pretty fast clip. I noticed the other day though, upon allowing a friend to park in my garage, I could see how slowly he parked in comparison to my speed. Notably, the first time involves wanting to make sure that you are getting a feel for where the car goes. After multiple such parking achievements, it becomes easier. A good AI component has this learning capability.

The self-driving car though cannot make an assumption that the garage parking situation is identical each time the self-driving car parks the car. For example, the other day, I opened my garage door and realized that one of my children had parked their bike into the spot where my car would normally go. If I had proceeded on the basis of my earlier learned static map of the garage, I would have run into the parked bicycle. As such, the self-driving car needs to re-assess each time, identifying whether the parking situation has changed from what it earlier knew.

For some homeowners, they put various devices into their garages to make parking easier to do. For example, a low-tech method involves hanging a tennis ball from a string, placing this into the middle of the garage to help a human driver realize they must park to the left or right of the hanging marker. There are more high-tech devices such as a signal light with a sensor. The signal light is hung onto a wall of the garage and shines the usual colors of green, yellow, red, and will then try to help guide you as a human to park your non-self-driving car.

Our viewpoint is that you should not need to trick-out your garage for purposes of having a self-driving car park into your garage. I realize that some auto makers are going to try and go this route, namely get owners of self-driving cars to buy special add-on devices that need to be mounted or placed into a garage, thereby allowing a "normal" self-driving car to park into the garage. We don't think this is needed and also view it as a brazen attempt at solving a problem by simply upselling the consumer.

The AI of the self-driving car should have the smarts needed to park that self-driving car into the garage, and no added gimmicks or expensive add-ons should be needed. Raise the bar on self-driving cars, we say, and not dumb them down.

CHAPTER 12
MOTIVATIONAL AI IRRATIONALITY FOR SELF-DRIVING CARS

CHAPTER 12

MOTIVATIONAL AI IRRATIONALITY FOR SELF-DRIVING CARS

What the heck is that person doing?

Have you ever been driving along and witnessed another driver that pulled some kind of seemingly crazy stunt? I am sure that you have. Seems like we all have. For most of our driving time, we see drivers doing normal, everyday, primarily rational acts in terms of abiding by the rules of the road and otherwise driving in a rational manner. On occasion, we see drivers that appear to have gone off the deep end. Their driving behavior is nutty, weird, off-the-wall, and what we might more formally call irrational.

Humans are supposed to be rational, according to dominant economic theories, and yet people often do irrational things. If people do indeed do irrational things, is it done on a random basis such that there is no means to anticipate in what ways they will be irrational? According to Richard Thaler, recent winner of the Noble Prize in Economic Sciences, people are predictably irrational. His work helped to spawn a subfield of economics that entails how human nature can be irrational and yet also be anticipated and dealt with.

Thaler's efforts and those of his colleagues represent an important extension to the earlier economic beliefs that people were near enough to being rational that having to deal with their irrational behavior was inconsequential. The irrational acts of people were considered a rounding error. If you could model the rational behavior of people, there was no need to take a look at their irrational efforts. The rational models presumed that such models captured 99% of what people did and the remaining 1% was inconsequential.

Furthermore, even if somehow the irrational behavior was more so than just the tiny percentage, some argued previously that even if you did want to bother with looking at irrational behavior, it would not have done you much good because the irrational was so random that you wouldn't be able to pin it down in any useful way anyhow. Why waste time studying something that would have no particular pattern to it? Without any discernible pattern, there was no means to make it fit into any kind of mathematical model of human behavior.

Notice too that there were some that at first even had said that people are either rational or they are irrational, but could not be both at the same time. In other words, out of a pool of say one hundred people, it used to be thought that maybe 95 of them are rational and there are perhaps 5 that are irrational. This though ultimately was shown to be misleading and misinformed. A person can switch from one state to another, being at one moment rational and the next moment irrational, and thus you cannot make some overarching assumption that people are always one way or the other. Each of us exhibits a mixture of both rational and irrational behaviors, and the emergence of rational or irrational behavior is dictated by numerous underlying factors such as the person, the context of the situation, and so on.

Here's something for you to ponder. Each morning, during my daily commute on the freeway, I am surrounded by hundreds of other cars throughout the stretch of my commute. Any of these other drivers could easily wreak havoc by ramming their car into other cars. Instead, we all generally seem to abide by the rules-of-the-road and avoid killing each other. We adjust to the start and stop nature of the traffic, we switch lanes without banging into each other, and otherwise undertake a delicate dance involving quite hefty killing machines that could readily harm others (our cars).

Sure, there are during my commute the fender benders, along with some even more serious accidents that occur. Those are primarily indeed "accidents" in that the drivers weren't paying attention to the driving situations, or were cutting things too close when making a lane shift. There are a few that are hampered by perhaps being drunk and so they bring about an accident. Overall, we would likely agree that most of the drivers for most of the time are acting in a rational manner.

This is somewhat startling when you think about it. Why is it that all these drivers are all abiding by rules that are in their heads and yet otherwise there is nothing that prevents them from just ramming their car into other cars? There is nothing built into any of these cars that prevents the driver from doing serious damage and destruction to others. If one of them wanted to start sideswiping other cars, they could do so. Think of the tremendous amount of trust that we all take into account when we get onto the roadways. We are making a fundamental life-or-death assumption that those people driving cars out there are going to do so in a primarily rational way. That's a huge assumption, in the sense of the risk to life and limb if that assumption is incorrect.

What motivates this rational behavior? One aspect could be self-preservation. Each driver realizes that if they ram into another car, there is the potential for themselves to be injured. Rational behavior says we don't normally want to harm ourselves. Another basis for this rational behavior is the potential personal cost to causing an accident, such as the possibility that you'll need to payout money to others due to having caused an accident. You don't want to lose your savings, your mortgage, and your other funds so you opt to try and avoid getting into an accident. Another might be that you don't want to go to jail. And so on.

One might also say that it is perhaps because people don't want to harm other people. This is at times though is argued as being a bit optimistic about people and some would say perhaps an overly altruistic viewpoint. It is heartwarming to think that other than the potential for personal penalties, such as being physically harmed yourself or losing your money or going to jail, you would want to also not cause harm to others. This could be claimed as a culturally derived aspect and be seen as a mental curse that if you do harm others that your mind will haunt you (and so, we are back to the self-preservation notion).

Given all the above about rational behavior, and the aspect that most of the time we see rational driving behavior, nonetheless we do witness irrational behavior while on the roads. The magnitude of the irrational behavior varies quite a bit, and thus sometimes we'll see small acts of irrational driving and at other times larger acts of irrational driving. The other day, a driver suddenly darted out of the car pool lane, doing so by illegally crossing the double yellow lines and not waiting for a legal portion to exit from the car pool lane, and then darted across all other four lanes of traffic to try and reach an upcoming freeway exit. The driver disrupted the flow of traffic and risked the lives of all other drivers nearby, along with the potential that had an accident occurred it could have caused a domino effect that would have harmed lots of other drivers behind us all. The move was reckless, illegal, irresponsible, outrageous, scary, unwarranted, and could have generated very adverse consequences.

Was the driver aware of the potential impact? Or, was the driver mentally unaware and was just acting on an impulse that they wanted to get to the freeway exit and so darted across all lanes of traffic with that one goal in mind? Did the driver calculate that they could do this darting and do so without harming anyone else and not putting themselves into harm? Or, did they do this act without any real anticipation of the impacts?

And, why should we care about rational versus irrational driving behavior?

At the Cybernetic Self-Driving Car Institute, we assert that self-driving cars will need to be aware of the rational and irrational driving behavior of human drivers in order to best navigate and maneuver in a world that is a mixture of self-driving cars and human driven cars. Furthermore, we assert that self-driving cars themselves have the potential to be susceptible to irrational behavior and that as AI developers we need to be cognizant of this aspect and deal with it accordingly.

First, in terms of being aware of human driving behavior, Thaler's indication that irrationality can be possibly predicted is quite helpful to the AI of the self-driving car. In my story above about the wild driver that cut across all lanes of traffic, you might at first say that this can happen at any time and that any driver might do the same, thus, presumably there is no means to accurately predict it. But, we suggest this is not always the case.

In fact, the driver that was in the car pool lane had been making motions that suggested an upcoming attempt at darting across the lanes might occur. They were very subtle signs. The driver was looking over their shoulder at the traffic to their right and kept moving their head back-and-forth. The car was edging onto the lane marker that divides the car pool lane from the next lane over. The driver was moving somewhat erratically in terms of rapidly accelerating up to the next car in the car pool lane and then shaving off distance, which might seem odd but was a potential effort to find a spot to exit out of the car pool lane.

If other drivers weren't paying attention to that particular car, from their perspective it was like a bolt of lightning out of the sky that the driver suddenly made the crazy maneuver. For those drivers that were watching his car closely, you could sense that something was afoot. There was just enough unusual actions that you kind of instinctively knew that something was going to happen. In my case, I was noticing the car because I like to watch traffic around me and detect patterns in driving. I'd guess that most of my fellow morning commuters are probably instead thinking about what they are going to do at work that day or where they will go for lunch that afternoon. I study drivers.

The point here is that we would want a truly good self-driving car to be able to spot those same subtle signs and be able to act accordingly. We would want the AI to be able to predict irrationality. A Level 5 self-driving car is supposed to do everything that a human driver could do when driving the self-driving car. Should the Level 5 self-driving car drive like an unaware driver or an aware driver? Our goal is to make a self-driving car that is the best driver that can possibly be provided. Some AI systems for self-driving cars might meet the test of being able to drive a self-driving car like a human does, but then fall below the capability of a versatile and savvy driver. We say that the goal should not be to just have AI that can drive a car like a human can, but drive a car like a really savvy human can.

Another factor about irrational behavior and self-driving cars is the role of the human occupant that is inside a self-driving car.

There are some self-driving car makers that are falsely believing that a human occupant in a self-driving car will only provide an indication of where to drive, and then the self-driving car AI does everything else. We have indicated over and over that the occupant is going to want to interact with the AI of the self-driving car, and in fact will need to interact with the self-driving car. There is a lot more to being an occupant than just saying where you want to go.

Occupants will want to potentially change the destination during the journey within the self-driving car. They might want the self-driving car to take a particular route, or change routes. They might want the self-driving car to go slowly and so the human can enjoy the view, or the human might be in a rush and want the self-driving car to go as fast as allowed. There are a myriad of reasons that the human occupants and the self-driving car will interact with each other.

Thaler's efforts of predicted irrationality can come to play in this.

Overconfidence effect.

When studying the NFL football draft, Thaler and his colleagues found that the professional football scouts tended to overweigh their judgement about players. The famous movie Moneyball showed similarly how in another sport, baseball, statistics could at times do a better job than could human judgement about the potential for various sports players.

We are anticipating that humans will at first tend to believe that their self-driving cars can do more than the self-driving car can actually do. Early adopters of self-driving cars are often over confident about what the self-driving car can do. There are lots of YouTube videos of Tesla drivers that take their hands off the wheel of the car and don't seem to realize they are placing themselves into enormous risk. This is in spite of being told by Tesla that they are not to take their hands off the wheels.

Notice that most of the emerging self-driving cars that are at the Levels 2 to 4 are requiring some form of detection mechanism to force the human driver to keep their hands on the wheel. This is a type of nudge. Thaler has argued that to get people toward rational behavior that we need to give them nudges toward it, shifting their irrational behavior over into rational behavior. We can predict that humans will do something irrational like taking their hands off the wheel of a car that is going 80 miles per hour and do so under the false assumption that the self-driving car will do the driving for them. Therefore, rather than just instructing people to not do this, we put in place a mechanism such as a device that detects when hands are not on the wheel and then blare a reminder to put your hands onto the wheel. If the person does not comply, some models of cars are even programmed to gradually slow down and come to a stop. This is a nudge.

Endowment Effect.

Thaler indicates that people tend to have an endowment effect, involving ownership of things. In his experiments, he had subjects buy a mug for $3 that then subsequently refused to sell it for $6. It would seem the right thing to have done would be to take the easy and quick profit by selling the mug for the six dollars. Thaler claims that people tend to add value to an object by the very fact that they believe they own the object.

For self-driving cars, we anticipate that owners of a self-driving car will potentially exhibit the same kind of endowment effect. They will get into their self-driving car, and upon going onto the roadways will believe that their car is superior to other cars. They will likely want their AI to drive accordingly. They will think that their self-driving car should somehow go faster, drive better, get them to their destination sooner, merely because it is a self-driving car and that they own it.

Fairness Effect.

Thaler found that people tended toward believing in fairness and refused to do something seemingly rational because of this notion. In one experiment, it was raining and so people would want to have an umbrella. When the store selling umbrellas rose the price by even a modest amount, doing so when it rained, the people that were going to buy an umbrella tended to not do so, even though they could have used it due to the rain. They felt they were being gouged and so in spite of now potentially getting wet in the rain, they preferred to do so rather than cave into the price gouging, even when the price itself was only marginally higher.

On the roadways, I continually witness drivers that get upset about a lack of fairness, in their viewpoint. For example, there is an offramp that I take most days, and it has a rightmost lane to turn right upon reaching the end of the offramp. There is a lane to the left, which is intended for those going straight or that want to turn left at the end of the offramp. There are drivers each morning that get into the lane that is intended to go straight or to turn left, and they suddenly want to squeeze into the lane that is intended to make a right turn.

This is upsetting to some drivers that are already in the right turn lane, since the driver in the other lane is appearing to be rudely "taking cuts" into the right turn lane. Some of those drivers taking cuts are perhaps innocent drivers that got confused and realized they needed to be in the rightmost lane. But, some of those drivers are perhaps seasoned drivers that really know that the rightmost lane backs up, and that they can devilishly go in the other lane and then try to barge into the rightmost lane. This allows them to reduce their wait time in the always overflowing rightmost lane.

I've seen many drivers in the rightmost lane that will do almost anything to prevent these intruder cars from getting into the rightmost lane. Perhaps due to a concern over fairness, the drivers are trying to prevent the cut taking drivers from getting into the lane. You could also say that the drivers preventing the cuts are trying to prevent themselves from having to wait longer, and so every time they see someone ahead of them allow a cut into the lane, it makes the wait time even longer. I am sure that the wait time is a factor, but I'd bet it is more about the fairness factor than the wait time per se.

How will a self-driving car handle these "fairness" situations. As an occupant in a self-driving car, you might become enraged to see that your self-driving car is letting all these interlopers into the rightmost lane. Your self-driving car is allowing the unfairness of others to be impinge on you. The odds are that you'll become upset with your AI and want it to help enforce greater fairness on the roadways. I know that some dreamers will be saying that once we have all self-driving cars that it will be easy to enforce this fairness, but I'd like to emphasize that it will be decades upon decades before we have all self-driving cars and no human driven cars. In essence, we are going to have a mix of self-driving cars and human driven cars for a very long time, and so the AI of the self-driving cars needs to be able to handle that mix.

We are making AI that interacts with the occupants of the self-driving car and can interpret driving commands in a fashion that is compatible with the roadway conditions and circumstances. The AI provides feedback to the occupant about what is feasible versus not feasible. And, we have the system provide a "nudge" to the occupant to get them to shift toward rational behavior if their requests appear to be of an irrational nature.

This brings up another facet of the AI, namely that it too can have its own motivations and be rational or irrational. I know that many of you will be shocked by such a statement. You are likely insistent that the AI would always be rational. It can never be irrational. We have grown up with so many movies and TV shows that depict robots and AI of the future that is purely without emotion and without any sense of irrational behavior.

It's a crock.

AI systems are being developed in a variety of ways, including via neural networks and other machine learning techniques. Via those black box style efforts, we don't know for sure why the AI will be doing what it does. Complex patterns are being automatically found and utilized via those automated methods, much of which is so complex that we don't have any direct means to have it explained by the AI. In that sense, as I've warned many times, we are going to have all sorts of inherent biases carried into our AI systems. It's a given.

This might not be the same kind of motivation that humans have, but it will be patterned upon that motivation. So, whether it exists due to some biological apparatus is not the key, instead we need to focus that it exists in the automation as a result of pattern matching across large data sets that subliminally contain that motivation.

We can also expect that the AI for any self-driving car is going to potentially take on the characteristics of the owner or occupants that go in that self-driving car. If we are going to have self-driving cars that learn over time, and each time they have a human occupant that we'll call Bob, presumably the AI will begin to learn what Bob likes and dislikes from a driving perspective. This makes sense that the AI would customize to the nature of the owner occupant. Auto makers will want to provide this capability and humans will certainly expect it.

As such, the AI will begin to absorb some of the aspects of the owner occupants. If Bob is the type of person that wants his car rides to be fast and furious, the AI in that self-driving car is going to likely try to achieve this. It will then become part and parcel of the means of how that AI is driving the self-driving car for that person. Furthermore, if the AI of that self-driving car is part of a collective of self-driving cars that share among each other, the driving behavior could be further distributed to other self-driving cars.

This also raises the question about the role of government in self-driving cars and the driving behavior of the AI. At some point, will the government opt to embed into the AI of the self-driving cars various aspects of what is rational driving behavior versus irrational? Right now, the AI makers for self-driving cars are mainly embedding the legal rules-of-the-road. Those are generally clear cut. The cultural aspects of driving are not so clearly written down and not so clearly specified. The government might want to put "nudges" into the AI of the self-driving cars that will shift the AI toward behavior that is considered preferred.

One aspect of Thaler's work that you might find especially intriguing is the men's urinal studies that he has done. For those of you that aren't aware, when men go into a public bathroom and use a urinal, they do so standing up and are intended to focus their output into the urinal. Unfortunately, many men seem to miss the mark and the floor around a urinal often becomes a slippery stinky mess (if you get my drift). In some urinals, they placed a small image of a fly, placed toward the center area of the urinal. Why was this done?

This was a nudge. Men were now motivated to aim toward the image of the fly. What fun! This more importantly got men to focus their widespread aim toward a specific target. According to the studies, this dramatically reduced the amount of spillover. We are going to likely see in self-driving cars and AI that there will be many instances of the need for "nudges" like this. It will be needed for purposes of having AI cope with the irrational human drivers on the roads, and for AI that becomes itself an irrational driver due to their learning from other drivers on the roads.

Finally, we also need to be wary of human occupants that want their self-driving cars to do untoward actions. For example, suppose someone is bent on killing themselves and they decide the easiest way to do so would be to have their self-driving car get into an accident while they are riding in the self-driving car. They might give commands to the self-driving car to purposely get it into a tight spot, one that could lead to death and destruction. This so-called "suicide by self-driving car" is something that has real potential and that we would want the AI to detect and prevent.

Self-driving cars need to be designed and built on the basis of being aware of rational behavior and irrational behavior. As per Thaler, there is predictable irrational behavior that we can anticipate and therefore cope with. Our AI systems need to be robust enough to deal with this. And, we will need to incorporate nudges into them too.

CHAPTER 13
CURIOUSITY AS COGNITION FOR SELF-DRIVING CARS

CHAPTER 13

CURIOUSITY AS COGNITION FOR SELF-DRIVING CARS

I live in a gated community that has a main gate for residents and guests, and provides an impressive driving entrance into the neighborhood that displays ornate iron gates and a spectacular water-sprouting fountain. There is a secondary gate at the back of the community. This secondary gate is intended for various contractors and vendors that need to gain access into the neighborhood and it also provides a fast way to get into and out of the neighborhood for the residents, though the gate is very simple in appearance and can be considered of utility value only. For many years, I've routinely used both the main gate and the secondary gate.

One day, I drove into the community via the main gate and wondered where some of the roads in the community led to. I usually just drive straight to my home and don't diverge from an otherwise highly efficient and optimized driving route from the gates to my home. Why bother, I had thought, in terms of exploring the rest of the neighborhood. I knew the aspects that I needed to know, namely, where my home is, and how to get into and out of the community. Nothing more to be concerned with, I figured.

As I drove down a winding road in the neighborhood, it gradually looked like it would reach presumably a dead-end at one of the edges of the surrounding protective fence. Instead, I discovered that there was a gate at the end of the road. The gate was nearly out of view and only those that likely lived on that particular street even knew it was there. A secret passage! I inched my car up to the gate and it opened, leading out to a public street that is seldom used. I felt like I was a secret agent that now knew of way to go into and out of the gated community virtually unseen. How exciting!

This story illustrates some interesting aspects. First, let's consider how I found this hidden treasure. Question for you — had I been focused on a goal to find another way into or out of the gated community? No. In fact, I was completely unaware that such a third gate even existed, which is kind of surprising since I had lived in this neighborhood for several years. You would have thought that I would have at some point either encountered the third gate, or maybe the guards at the other two gates would have mentioned it, or my neighbors would have said something about it, etc.

What was it then that led to the discovery? Answer: my curiosity. I was just generally curious about the community and happened to have some spare time to indulge my curiosity. I really had no idea what I might find by driving around somewhat aimlessly. If you had asked me beforehand, I would have bet that I wouldn't find anything particularly interesting. I assumed it would be just home upon home, all pretty much looking the same. Nowhere in my mind was the idea that I would find another gate.

It was my curiosity that caused me to look around. It was curiosity that led to this surprising and quite helpful discovery. Without that curiosity, I would have remained blissfully unaware of the discovery and not have been the wiser that it existed. Though I admit that this discovery was not as though I had found a new subatomic particle or that there are aliens from Mars here on our planet, it was nonetheless a productive result of my curiosity.

You might be aware of the famous quote by Albert Einstein about curiosity: "I have no special talent. I am only passionately curious." I think we might all agree that his modesty about not having any kind of special talent is a bit over-the-top in terms of humility, but anyway, we would likely all agree that he definitely had a large heaping of curiosity. Talent that has no curiosity is bound to be kept in a cage and not going to reach its true potential. Curiosity alone, without any kind of talent, probably would be somewhat wasted or might lead to troubles.

We all know that curiosity killed the cat, or so they say. That's why cats seem to have nine lives. Being curious is both an advantage and a disadvantage. A person that uses curiosity can make new discoveries, similar to what happened with my finding the third gate in my community. Of course, there was perhaps a chance too that my curiosity might have led to some calamity. Suppose I had driven down a street that had a group of thugs waiting for someone to unknowingly drive along, and they were waiting to stop the car and beat the driver to a pulp. In that case, I would have been cursing my curiosity.

In the case of my driving around the neighborhood, I had somewhat calculated the risks associated with indulging my curiosity. Where I live, the odds of a pack of thugs is close to zero, so that really wasn't an event that would occur (well, I did have a bunch of rambunctious children one day toss water balloons at my car, but I dare say those aren't thugs by the strict definition of the word). I did waste some of my personal time by driving around, and presumably could have used that time for some other purpose. I did use up some gasoline as I drove around, plus I was putting more wear and tear on my car. All of those costs, or one might say are disadvantages associated with my application of curiosity in this instance, but they were relatively mild, and so the opportunity (or advantages) to see the neighborhood and take a chance on finding whatever I might find was a reasonable one.

I have explained here that curiosity can be a carefully utilized tool that is chosen from a cognitive toolkit by using reasoning about the potential Return On Investment (ROI) of deploying the curiosity. That's not always the case that someone or something opts to presumably do an elaborate ROI calculation before invoking curiosity. Does a cat that leaps from the top shelf onto a nearby table in order to explore the table make use of a mental calculus about the motivations of curiosity? We don't know, but maybe it is fair to suggest that if there is some kind of calculus, it probably involves limited formulas. It might be a simplistic calculation of seeing something that catches the eye of the cat and so it then opts to go for it. If you watch cats carefully, you'll notice that they do seem to try and be a bit more elaborate in gauging the use of their curiosity, such as looking around first to see if there might be an obvious danger sitting on the table or that they don't have solid enough footing on the shelve to make the jump.

For humans, we generally believe that curiosity is crucial for human development. Research in psychology and also in neuroscience is replete with studies that purport to show the importance of curiosity in how we learn. Curiosity is considered a cornerstone for doing explorations of our world around us, and for the desire to formulate hypotheses and test them to see where they lead. Some argue that curiosity is found in all animals, and that in humans we take it to another higher level of usage by being able to increase our knowledge and insights. At times, humans exhibit perhaps the same basic level of curiosity and get the same benefits (and costs) as animals, such as the human that leaps from the top of his house over to a nearby tree to see if it can be done (saw this on YouTube, somewhat like my earlier indication of a leaping cat), but at the same time we have instances such as Albert Einstein that leveraged curiosity to find new ways to describe our understanding of energy and matter. It seems doubtful that many cats or even dogs can use curiosity in quite that same way as Einstein did.

You can think of curiosity as typically depicted as being either so-called "state curiosity" or being "trait curiosity." State curiosity is the type of curiosity that seeks to employ curiosity simply for the sake of using curiosity. If I have curiosity, I might use it because I can. Perhaps I have no particular goal in mind for using the curiosity. I just let it run its course. In the case of my story about the gated community, you could say that perhaps I was making use of state curiosity and driving around just out of overall curiosity.

In the case of trait curiosity, there is supposedly some form of learning goal that underlies the use of the curiosity. Let's say that in the case of the gated community, I had wanted to know where each of the roads led, as a precaution if I should ever get lost in the neighborhood and wanted to have an already formulated map of the streets. In that scenario, my curiosity had a particular focus of learning. I knew that I wanted to create a map of the community and my curiosity spurred me to do so.

It can be a fine line between the state curiosity and trait curiosity. At one moment, my curiosity is being spurred by this desire to make a map, and the next moment I come upon the third gate. If I was strictly focused on only making the map, I probably would have not tried to use the gate and instead merely continued driving around. In short, there are times at which curiosity can be a mixture of state and trait, and they can intertwine around each other in a fluid fashion.

In the field of AI, we are quite interested in curiosity. Why so? Well, if you believe that human intelligence depends to some extent on the cognitive aspects and capabilities of curiosity, and if you are trying to create artificial intelligence that is based on what human intelligence consists of, you naturally would want to know how curiosity works. By figuring out how curiosity works in human intelligence, you could try to mimic it in a machine and then maybe that helps to produce a true AI system. Can humans exist without curiosity and be considered intelligent? If so, then presumably AI wouldn't need any semblance of curiosity in order to be as intelligent as humans. On the other hand, it does seem like curiosity is pretty commonly found in humans, whether innately or learned, we aren't quite sure, but anyway it is present and so we in the AI field believe it worthy to pursue it.

Curiosity at times could be viewed as a means of reducing uncertainty. There is uncertainty in your environment and thus you use curiosity to reduce that uncertainty. My uncertainty was about the roads and nuances of my gated community. I reduced my uncertainty by driving around. Or, you could say that I increased my certainty about my environment. I became more certain about what was there. This could be a means to boost my chances of survival, allowing me to be better able to survive in my environment. If you are familiar with Maslow's hierarchy, you could say that curiosity can have a payoff at any level of the hierarchy, and not just be solely a benefit for the survival level of the human condition.

You could also claim that curiosity allows humans to seek new opportunities. One theory called the optimal-arousal theory posits that we use curiosity for finding something that can gain us an advantage of some kind. My curiosity about my gated community could have been due to my desire to find a better house and maybe during my driving around I'd find a house for sale that I otherwise did not know about. Rather than looking at curiosity as reducing uncertainty, this theory is a camp that asserts we use curiosity to gain new ground.

The neuroscientists and biologists and chemists might say that curiosity is driven by our neurotransmitters. There seems to be evidence to suggest that indulging your curiosity can release dopamine and opioids. You could say that we have curiosity and use our curiosity as a pleasure seeking animalistic mechanism. Just like your enjoying ice cream on a hot day, your curiosity is a satisfier that causes your human body and your human mind to have a good time.

In the above sense of reducing uncertainty, of seeking opportunities, of wanting to be pleased, AI tends to so far be modeling curiosity as a rewards and penalties type of mathematical function. For example, researchers Pulkit Agrawal, Deepak Pathak, Alexei Efros, and Trevor Darrell at the University of California Berkeley AI Research Lab have explored how curiosity works by establishing an elaborate points system for rewarding successful behaviors and for penalizing unwanted behaviors, doing so in such tasks as an AI system learning to play the video game of Super Mario Brothers. Some characterize this as a carrot-and-stick approach to doing machine learning. Underlying this application of curiosity is the notion of bounding the curiosity by both intrinsic motivation and by extrinsic motivation.

What does all of this discussion here about curiosity have to do with self-driving cars? At the Cybernetic Self-Driving Car Institute, we are developing software components that go into a self-driving car application portfolio and provide an added cognitive capability shaped around curiosity. In essence, we want to provide self-driving cars with a cognitive tool consisting of curiosity.

You might be surprised to hear this. What, you say, a self-driving car being curious? Crazy idea, you might at first suggest. Well, remember earlier when I mentioned the idea that curiosity seems to be an essential element of human intelligence, and that AI if it is to be considered equivalent to human intelligence we might therefore need to embody curiosity into AI – let's tie that aspect to the fact that a

NEW ADVANCES IN AI AUTONOMOUS DRIVERLESS SELF-DRIVING CARS

Level 5 self-driving car is supposed to be able to drive a car in whatever manner that a human could drive a car. For the AI to do so, it can be argued that the AI needs to thusly have curiosity.

When I have given presentations about our self-driving car "curiosity invoking" software component, I've had some that tried to instantly discount the idea, doing so by saying that if a self-driving car got curious, maybe it would wonder what it is like to drive off the end of a pier, and the next thing you know, a self-driving car full of human occupants decides to drive off the end of the nearest pier. I get that point, and I would also say that's a pretty stupid implementation of curiosity. In that sense, I agree that we don't want unbounded curiosity in our AI.

This is true pretty much of any AI that uses curiosity. You likely don't want the curiosity to run unbounded and unfettered. You could certainly also make the same case about humans and animals. If a human or an animal allowed curiosity to get the better of itself, you'd indeed have a many a case of the infamous curiosity that killed the cat. Indeed, there are daily stories in the news about people that did something untoward, presumably allowing their curiosity to go wild, and get themselves into really bad situations. The other day, a man was curious about where his toilet pipe led to, and so he reached in with his arm and got stuck. They had to break apart the toilet to get his arm out. Not the best use of curiosity, I'd say.

Our curiosity software for self-driving cars is bounded by parameters that avoid aspects such as getting curious about driving off a pier, or any similar kind of dangerous or ill-advised action. There are "curiosity traps" that we know to be watchful for about making use of curiosity. For example, curiosity can be excessive, and as such the cost can exceed the benefit of invoking it. If I had driven around in my gated community endlessly, it would have been an of excess curiosity and gotten the better of me. Curiosity can also lead to dead-ends, and as such, this also needs to be detected.

The way we've been developing the cognitive curiosity capability involves self-curiosity and also human-directed curiosity.

In the case of self-curiosity, the AI seeks to employ curiosity on its own, without a human urging it to do so. We continually have the curiosity component running in background, and it then shares what it finds with the other components, such as the self-driving car strategic AI component and the tactical components, which then can decide whether to make use of what the curiosity component has found.

For example, the curiosity component is looking at the path that the self-driving car is taking, and seeking to identify alternative paths. This is more than the already traditional approach of finding paths that are better optimized paths. Our curiosity component is looking at other paths that aren't necessarily more optimized for route planning purposes. Instead, these other paths might offer some other valued aspect, such as a more scenic route, or a route that could be later used when traffic is snarled.

It also is observing other cars in the surrounding environment, and trying to figure out what those cars are up to. As I've mentioned in my other writings, self-driving cars can be enhanced by how they observe and potentially learn from other cars, whether other human driven cars or self-driving cars. The curiosity component is peeking at the sensor data and sensor fusion of the self-driving car, and trying to spot seemingly curious behaviors of other cars, which then it can bring to the attention of the other elements of the self-driving car that are strategically and tactically driving the self-driving car.

In addition to self-curiosity, there is also human-directed curiosity. The human in the self-driving car is able to interact with the component dealing with curiosity, and inspire or help shape the focus of the curiosity component. If I were in the self-driving car as an occupant, I might encourage the self-driving car to take its time getting to my destination and show me around to some novel places. The curiosity tool then overtly gets invoked and becomes a key component for what the self-driving car creates as the traversal plan.

There are some that believe our self-driving cars will be working all the time, meaning that even when you as the owner aren't in the self-driving car, it nonetheless might be driving around. One reason for the self-driving car to be driving around involves the notion that we might all become Uber-like and have our self-driving cars be doing ride-sharing when we are not using the self-driving car. Another less obvious aspect involves having your self-driving car learn more about its environment, doing so without you needing to be in the self-driving car. Imagine, for example, if I had a self-driving car that I had parked at my home in my gated community. It might have on its own opted to explore my gated community and found the third gate (self-curiosity), or I might have tasked the self-driving car to go ahead and drive around and let me know what it finds (spurring the curiosity component to the forefront via human-directed curiosity).

Curiosity can be focused or unfocused. It can be working in the background in case it finds something worthy of consideration, or it can be at the forefront. It needs to be roped in and not allowed to overtake the rest of the system. The ROI for making use of curiosity has to be kept in mind and be an overt aspect of weighing the value of deploying curiosity or not, and the context and situation will all be factors that can shape the circumstance of when curiosity makes sense to use or not.

We believe that curiosity is and will be an essential tool in self-driving cars. Whether you agree or not to that notion, I think that at least you might agree that curiosity as an essential element in AI has merits. Let's all use our curiosity to at least see how we can further extend AI to embody curiosity. I hope I've piqued your curiosity to do so!

CHAPTER 14
AUTOMOTIVES RECALLS OF SELF-DRIVING CARS

CHAPTER 14

AUTOMOTIVE RECALLS OF SELF-DRIVING CARS

The other day I took my car into my local dealership for an oil change and some other minor maintenance work. Upon doing so, the dealer looked up my car in a special database and discovered that there was a recall on my transmission. The dealer asked me why I had not brought the car in sooner, since the recall was about a year old. I protested that I had no inkling that there was a recall involving my car. Further inspection of the database revealed that a letter from the auto maker was sent to me via the good old US postal service, but the address on file was an outdated one. Undoubtedly, the recall notice went to that address and the person there tossed it away as so much junk mail.

Little did that person know that they might have sealed my fate. Suppose the recall was a very serious and imminently endangering fault or flaw in my car? I could have been driving along on a beautiful countryside winding road, and all of a sudden my transmission gives out. Next thing you know, the car goes nuts and no matter what kind of evasive action I take, the car barrels into a fence and strikes a herd of cows. Well, maybe that's a bit dramatic, but you get my drift. The aspect that the car had a recall was important for me to know, and likewise doing something about the recall would usually be prudent, since it is a matter of the safety of the car and therefore the safety of those driving the car or being occupants in the car.

Here's a staggering statistic for you about automotive recalls. There were about 53 million car recalls in the United States last year.

Think about that for a moment. Since there are about 200 million cars in the United States, the stat about last year's recalls means that nearly one-fourth of all cars were encompassed by a recall. Another way to envision this would be to look at your car and if there are three other cars parked next to your car, one of those four cars has a recall on it. Ouch! That's a lot of recalls. There were about 1,000 recall campaigns last year, meaning that the auto makers identified about a thousand separate recalls and for which the total number of cars impacted was the 53 million cars that came under the recalls.

Sometimes an automotive recall is widespread, while in other cases it is relatively narrow.

Let's review some of the famous and most widespread recalls. Probably the one that we all have heard recently the most about involves the Takata airbags. This case involved faulty airbag inflators. The danger associated with the fault was that the airbag could rupture upon being inflated, and then it would potentially spew metallic fragments at the driver and occupants of the car. Imagine shrapnel from a bomb, and that's about what it was doing. The recall started in 2013 and involved nearly 70 million cars. Part of the reason that so many cars were involved was due to the aspect that over 20 auto makers had opted to use the Takata airbags in their vehicles. The number of recalls can get pretty high when the component being recalled is something that multiple auto makers have decided to use in their cars.

A notable recall that involved a smaller number of cars but that got tremendous attention involved faulty ignition switches in various GM (General Motors) cars. Investigations showed that the ignition switch could slip out of the normal engagement mode while the car was actively running and abruptly jump into accessory mode. Doing so would cause the engine to shut down, along with cutting off power, and led to hundreds of people suffering injuries or deaths due to the fault occurring at the wrong time in the wrong place. This recall involved "only" about six million cars. The lethal nature of it and the fact that it had occurred repeatedly made this recall especially notable. In addition, when it became known that the defect existed, there was a big scandal when it was discovered that GM had tried to hide the problem and had not taken proper and prompt action about the recall.

According to the US governmental agency known as the National Highway Traffic Safety Administration (NHTSA): "A recall is issued when a manufacturer or NHTSA determines that a vehicle, equipment, car seat, or tire creates an unreasonable safety risk or fails to meet minimum safety standards. Most decisions to conduct a recall and remedy a safety defect are made voluntarily by manufacturers prior to any involvement by NHTSA. Manufacturers are required to fix the problem by repairing it, replacing it, offering a refund, or in rare cases repurchasing the vehicle."

In one sense, you could say that there is a bit of a game that is played by auto makers.

They are supposed to voluntarily be proactive and try to identify when a recall is needed, and then take proper action about the recall. Currently, the NHTSA regulations indicate that "Manufacturers will notify registered owners by first class mail within 60 days of notifying NHTSA of a recall decision. Manufacturers should offer a proper remedy to the owner." In theory, an auto maker will do the right thing, they will dutifully be on the watch for faults or problems that involve doing a recall, they will quickly act to undertake the recall, they will try earnestly to contact those impacted by the recall, and they will ensure that there is a remedy that can be readily applied for the recall.

Of course, not all auto makers will act in such an idealized manner. Some might not be watching for faults that are a sign of a need for a recall. Some might ignore faults that are brought to their attention. Some might try to do a cover-up and act like there isn't a fault and thus no need for a recall. Keep in mind that an auto maker will be looking at quite a cost to deal with a recall, since they will need to provide a replacement or fix to however many cars are impacted. This cost is bound to hurt their profits. Furthermore, they realize that the mere act of announcing a recall can also hurt their sales, including sales for the car models directly impacted, along with all of their other car models since consumers might believe that all cars from that auto maker are faulty.

If an auto maker drags their feet about a recall, on the one hand it could be handy for that auto maker in the short-term since it delays the potential impact of the recall from a cost and immediate public relations blowout perspective. But, if they get caught about having done little or even covered-up, there are chances that it could become an even worse public relations nightmare and even a costlier issue. There could also be the potential for criminal charges against the company and those that knew about the dangers and did nothing or covered-up the matter. And, let's not forget about the loss of lives that can occur because of a faulty aspect on a car.

What does any of this have to do with self-driving cars?

At the Cybernetic Self-Driving Car Institute, we have been pointing out that there are going to be automotive recalls involving self-driving cars. This sometimes catches some of the self-driving car pundits by surprise. They seem to be living in a nirvana world that includes the fanciful belief that self-driving cars will never break down and never have any faults or issues. It is both disheartening and scary that there are some so fervent over self-driving cars that they actually seem to believe that self-driving cars are going to be utterly error free.

It's a crock.

First of all, a self-driving car is still a car. By this I mean that it still has all of the normal aspects of a car, including that it has an engine, a transmission, tires, etc. All of those are components that today are subject to faults and failures, and will continue to be subject to faults and failures. We are going to have recalls on those aspects of self-driving cars. There isn't some magic fairy dust that just because the car is a self-driving car that all of those automotive parts are going to never fail. They will fail.

Next, we need to consider the specialized components that are going to be in a self-driving car. There will be lots of new hardware involved, including LIDAR devices, radar devices, sonar devices, cameras, and so on. This adds lots and lots of opportunity for mechanical and physical faults and failures. In essence, we can anticipate that a self-driving car is likely to have even more chances of a recall than a normal car, due to the addition of all of this nifty new hardware.

Another aspect will include the hundreds of likely microprocessors needed to underlie the AI and smarts of a self-driving car. We could have recalls impacting those microprocessors. Many of those microprocessors will be very specialized and have been made for the specific purposes of aiding a self-driving car. In that sense, they will not have stood the test of time in terms of being generalized microprocessors that have been in say our mobile phones and laptops. Their specialization will make them relatively unique, new, and generally untested in the field.

There is also the opportunity for a recall on the software of the self-driving car. There could be defects in the software that need to be fixed or replaced. Think about all of the defects in Microsoft Windows and you'll know what I mean when I say that we need to be realistic and assume there will be lots of defects in the software that runs and controls a self-driving car.

For the software recalls, I realize that many of you are likely saying to yourself that those can be fixed "easily" by doing an over-the-air replacement. Just as Tesla today does fixes for its car software by pushing new updates directly to the car in an Internet-like way, so too we should anticipate that most self-driving cars will be able to equally be fixed remotely in terms of the software.

This is both a yes and a no. Yes, in theory, the auto maker should be able to push patches and updates to the self-driving car and thus not need to physically have the self-driving car come to a place to have the software fixed. The no is that doing so will require remote access to the self-driving car, and there might be instances whereby the remote access cannot occur or is limited. For example, suppose the self-driving car is in a location that does not lend itself to remote access. Or, suppose that the communications components of the self-driving car are failing and it cannot do external communication. Admittedly, those will be rarer circumstances, but I am just pointing out that there are exceptions to the notion of readily doing software updates over-the-air.

Some potential twists that can help with recalls are indeed possible in an era of self-driving cars.

For example, I had mentioned in my story earlier about my transmission having a recall and that I was not aware that the recall even existed. This was due to the auto maker sending a snail mail notification to me, which I never received. With self-driving cars, presumably the auto maker can notify me more directly via my self-driving car. In essence, the auto maker informs my self-driving car, and it then informs me upon my next encounter with my self-driving car, such as when I get into it to go to the grocery store, it might verbally tell me that there is a recall on the transmission or whatever.

You could go even further and anticipate that the self-driving car might take itself in for the recall. Suppose that I am not going to be using my self-driving car for the next day or two, and it might then self-drive itself to the dealership. At the dealership, they replace the recalled part, and then they send the self-driving car back to me. All of this being done without my having to drive the car. Instead, the self-driving car goes to get the recall part replaced or fixed, and then drives itself back to me. That's nice!

There's another interesting aspect too that we'll likely see.

With GM's Chevrolet Bolt electrical vehicle, they recently were able to use their over-the-air telematics to remotely detect a battery related problem in some of the vehicles. It turns out that some of the Bolt EV's were misreporting the battery levels and causing human drivers to believe that there were more miles available to go than were actually available (the Bolt has an advertised range of 238 miles on a single full-battery charge). Not all of the Bolt EV's were having this issue. Normally, GM would have had all of the car owners take the car into a dealership to diagnose whether their particular car was one of the ones impacted. Instead, in this case, they were able to remotely detect which cars had the specific problem.

For situations wherein it is a software specific problem, as mentioned previously, presumably a software update can be remotely applied. Suppose though that it is a problem of a hardware nature?

In some cases, it might be possible to adjust the software (doing so remotely) to accommodate a hardware fault. If the ignition switch can slip from one status into another, such as the example mentioned earlier, suppose the software was updated to deal with the situation. Maybe the software could override a physical movement of the ignition switch, and decide that if the engine was running and the car was in motion that it made no sense to suddenly switch into the car accessory mode. Thus, a software related "workaround" might be possible when dealing with certain kinds of hardware or physical related faults.

We need to be mindful though that if a self-driving car has various software workarounds to contend with various hardware faults, it might not be prudent over the long term to just allow those hardware faults to continue to exist. It could be that the software workarounds are short-term measures to keep a self-driving car viably in action. You might think of this as the same as having run-flat tires, yes, you can still drive a car while using run-flat tires when you have a flat, but you should replace the tires with proper ones when you get the next chance to do so. Likewise, for some kinds of car parts that are faulty, even if the software can act as a workaround, it might still be needed to ultimately replace the faulty part.

Another aspect to consider about self-driving cars will be the safety of the driving of the car, under circumstances of parts recalls. When a human is informed about a recall for a conventional car, they might decide it isn't safe to drive the conventional car, and therefore have it towed to a dealership to make the needed repairs. For a self-driving car of a Level 5, will the AI be able to make a similar kind of determination? If it alone is informed about a recall, is it able or even right that it would somehow make that decision? Furthermore, suppose an AI driving self-driving car tries to drive even though the fault has serious potential repercussions?

If that seems a bit like a quandary, it is one that we definitely need to figure out and not just allow auto makers to decide arbitrarily. By the way, once we have self-driving cars, I would anticipate we'll have self-driving tow trucks. Thus, your self-driving car, which maybe should not be driving itself to the dealership for a recall, could have a self-driving tow truck that comes over, hooks up to the self-driving car, and takes it over to the dealership for you. That seems like a nice way to deal with things, avoiding having to get involved as a human per se. But, I point out, those same self-driving tow trucks might also be prowling neighborhoods and city streets looking for illegally parked cars, then automatically tow those to the police impound. Imagine that those self-driving tow trucks can do this twenty-four hours a day, seven days a week. For those of you that are scofflaws about where you park, this might not seem very dreamy.

Anyway, the emphasis here has been that we will have recalls that impact self-driving cars. They are cars. They will be subject to parts that are badly manufactured or otherwise have some kind of issues or faults. Furthermore, with the added components to make the car become a self-driving car, the odds of having a recall goes up. Those components, especially the hardware ones, are bound to also have some kinds of faults or failures. I don't want to seem like the bearer of bad news, but the notion that there will be no recalls is out-the-window, and even that there might be less recalls seems somewhat farfetched, though the aspect of communicating about recalls will certainly be improved as will at times the ability to workaround a recall or have the self-driving car itself go in automatically to take care of a recall.

CHAPTER 15
INTERNATIONALIZING AI FOR SELF-DRIVING CARS

CHAPTER 15
INTERNATIONALIZING AI
FOR
SELF-DRIVING CARS

Earlier in my career, I was a software engineer doing work for a global company that was based in New York and had offices in at least thirty other countries. While working on a new piece of software for the company, I was told somewhat after-the-fact that the software would eventually be used by non-English speakers and that it had to be ready-to-go in all of our other countries. We had offices in Germany, France, Britain, Netherlands, and so on. We also had offices in Japan, South Korea, China, and various other Asian locales. Thus, the languages were different and even the character sets used to express the languages were different. So much for having the actual needed requirements upfront before we started writing the code. I figured this new requirement would entail a rather sizable rewriting effort. Sigh.

My software development manager shrugged off the request and told me that this was a no-brainer request. He indicated that all we would need to do is invoke the double-byte capability of the compiler and then get someone to translate the text being displayed on the screens and reports, and voila the program would be perfectly suited for any of the other countries and languages that would use the software.

I fell for this on a classic "hook, line, and sinker" basis, in that I didn't really want to have to do any kind of a massive rewrite anyway, and thus the idea that it was flip-a-switch approach sounded pretty good to me. Perhaps as a young software engineer I had a bit too much exuberance and willingness to accept authority, I suppose.

We opted to use a system-based text translator to get the English into other tongues, rather than hiring a human to do the translations. This seemed easy and cheap as a means of getting the text into other languages. We translated all of the text being used in the program and stored those translations into tables. The program would merely ask at startup what language the person wanted to use, and from then on the program would select from the appropriate translated text stored in the tables in the code. When we tested the program, we assumed that the internationalizing of it was good, and did not actually try it out, and only had English-speaking users be our testers. Once the English-speakers gave us the thumbs up that the program was working correctly, we let everyone know it was ready for a full global rollout.

And sure enough, a fiasco and chaos ensued.

The auto-converter had done a lousy job of figuring out the semantics of the English text and how to best translate it into another language. It was one of those proverbial circumstances of text conversion seemingly gone mad. If you've ever read a Fortune Cookie message and laughed at the translation, you know what I mean about bad text translations. I remember one foreign hotel I stayed in that had a sign at the lobby check-in desk that said hotel guests were expected to complain at the front desk between the hours of 8:00 a.m. and 10:00 a.m. each day, implying that we were obligated to do so, rather than clarifying that if we had a complaint that it was that time of the day in which we could share it. That's how the auto-converter had translated a lot of the text in the program.

Not only was the text poorly translated, it turns out that the screens looked all messed-up due to the text being either longer or shorter than what the screen mock-ups had been. We had very carefully ensured that in English the screen text was well aligned, doing so both vertically and horizontally on the screen. There had been much effort put into making sure that the screen was crisp looking and easy to understand. With the translated text varying in sizes, it moved things around on the screen and looked like a mess.

The canned reports that we had developed came out the same messed-up kind of way. Columns no longer were in their proper place due to headers that pushed things over in one direction or another because the text for the headers now was varying in sizes as based on the language being used. Furthermore, a few of the reports turned out to have a mixture of English and the other languages being used, since the user could input text and we had assumed that any user that entered text would be entirely entering the text in their own language. Some of the users typed in text in English, even though the program thought it was supposed to be using receiving the chosen language such as say German. The program wasn't setup to translate the entered text, which some users assumed that the program would do for them.

We also discovered that the colors and various images used on the screens were not good choices for some of the countries. There were some countries that had various customs and cultural practices that the program did not properly abide by in terms of images shown and colors used.

We also had a part of the program that entered time for labor time tracking purposes and it too had missed the boat in terms of cultural differences. It allowed for entry on the basis of rounded hours, for example that you worked for 1 hour, 2 hours, and so on. In some of the countries, they kept track of hours to a fraction of an hour, either due to regulatory requirements or due to country customary practices. Thus, they wanted to enter 1.5 hours or 1.2 hours, but the program automatically rounded the entry to the nearest highest next number of hours. This was very frustrating for those countries and users, and also made turmoil out of how they were doing time tracking.

I suppose it is possible to look back and find this to be a rather quaint and humorous story. You can imagine that at the time, nobody was seeing much humor in any of this. There was a tremendous amount of finger-pointing that took place. Who had approved this lousy implementation for internationalization of the program? Why hadn't a more thoughtful approach been taken to it? How soon could a properly done internationalized version be rolled out? How could we be sure that the new version was accurately able to handle the international aspects of usage?

What does this have to do with self-driving cars?

At the Cybernetic Self-Driving Car Institute, we are working on making sure that the AI for self-driving cars is internationalized.

I am sure that you are thinking this must be a no-brainer. Similar to my story herein, isn't the internationalization of a self-driving car simply a flip-the-switch kind of effort? Sadly, many of the companies making self-driving car software are either not considering the internationalization of their systems, or they are assuming that once they've got it all perfected in the United States that it will be a breeze to convert it over to be used in other countries.

They are in for quite a shock.

This mindset is frequently seen in the United States. Make software that works here, and we pretty much figure it will be an easy knock-off to get it to work elsewhere. No provision is put toward preparing for that future. Instead, toss the work of it onto the backs of whomever comes along later on and wants it to be internationalized. I certainly do have sympathy for the system developers too, since they are often under the gun to get the system running, and trying to explain that it is taking you a bit longer because you are trying to infuse internationalization into it will not get you much leeway. We'll worry about that later, is the usual mantra from the top of the corporate ladder.

I had one software developer that is doing work for a major auto company that told me the only difference between what they are developing now in the United States and what will need to be redone in other countries is the roadway signs translations. In other words, he figured that the word "Stop" on a stop sign would need to be translated, and that otherwise the whole self-driving car was pretty much ready to go in other countries.

NEW ADVANCES IN AI AUTONOMOUS DRIVERLESS SELF-DRIVING CARS

We've been looking closely at what it takes to really and in a practical way have self-driving cars work in other countries besides the United States. It is a whole lot more than merely translating street signs.

There is an entire infusion of country customs and practices that need to be embodied throughout the self-driving car systems and its AI.

Let's consider Japan as an example.

The roads in Japan tend to be narrower than the roads are in the United States. You might at first figure that a road is a road, in that whether it is narrower or wider shouldn't make any difference to a self-driving car. Stay within your lanes, and it doesn't seem to matter if the road width is tight or wide. Not so.

If the AI of the self-driving car has "learned" about driving on United States roads, for example by using massive sets of driving data to train neural networks, those neural networks have as a hidden assumption aspects about the widths of the roadway. They have gotten infused within the system that there is a certain available latitude to vary within a lane, allowing the self-driving car to veer within the lane by a particular tolerance. This kind of tolerance for Japanese roads tends to be much tighter than the norm in the United States. The AI of the self-driving car will not necessarily realize (when suddenly plopped down in Japan) that there is an ongoing need to be more careful about maneuvers within its lane and as it goes into other lanes.

Another aspect relatively common in Japan consists of bicycle riders that tend to be somewhat careless and meander into car traffic when in the at-times crowded city driving environs. For those of you in the United States that have been to New York City, you've likely seen bike riding messengers that think they are cars and weave throughout car traffic. Multiply that tenfold and you've got a city like Tokyo. Why does this make a difference? The AI for a self-driving car in the United States would tend to assume that a bike rider is not going to become a key factor during driving of the car. Meanwhile, in Japan, detecting the presence of the bike riders is crucial, along with predicting what they will do next, and then have the AI contend with those aspects. This is not something that U.S. based self-driving car makers are particularly caring about right now.

Other more apparent differences exist too, of course. Drivers in Japan are seated on the right side of the car and traffic moves on the left. This does require changing key aspects of some of the core systems within the self-driving car AI. Right turns at red lights are generally not allowed, though again this is also something that a self-driving car in the United States would usually be properly programmed to handle (we have by-and-large right-turn-on-red, but there are exceptions).

Speaking of roadway signs, sometimes signs in Japan are intentionally translated into English so that visitors will be able to hopefully comprehend an important sign that otherwise is shown only in the native language. One of my favorites consists of a detour sign that said "Stop: Drive Sideways," which is a great example of how sometimes translations are amiss (do we need to make a self-driving car that can drive sideways?). Another example that has been reported in the news consisted of this alleged narrative on a car rental brochure in Tokyo: "When passenger of foot heave in sight, tootle the horn. Trumpet him melodiously at first, but if he still obstacles your passage then tootle him with vigor."

Continuing the aspects of internationalizing, there are other illustrative aspects about driving in Japan that further highlight the self-driving car aspects that need to be considered. For example, the roads in many parts of Japan tend to be rougher due to the frequent seismic movement and so the self-driving car is likely to get bounced around a lot. Are the sensors on the self-driving car ready for this kind of frequent and common place jarring? On some of the self-driving cars being tested today, the sensors are very fragile and I doubt they can handle a barrage of bumps and jarring, along with whether even the sensors will be able to collect crisp data for purposes of sensor fusion.

Most of the highways in Japan tend to be toll roads. I've previously discussed at some length the aspects of having self-driving cars deal with toll roads. If a self-driving car is at a Level 5, it means that the AI should be able to drive in whatever circumstances a human driver can drive. When it comes to toll roads, right now, most of the auto makers and tech companies making self-driving cars are assuming that the self-driving car will let the human occupant deal with the toll road specifics. This though can't be the case presumably for a true Level 5 self-driving car.

Another aspect in Japan is that there tends to be a lot of speeding through red lights at intersections once the light has gone red. Certainly the same kind of thing happens in the United States, but it often seems to be more prevalent in Japan. The AI of a self-driving car needs to consider how to handle this aspect, which is going to be recurring frequently while driving in Japan. The cars coming behind the self-driving car are going to want the self-driving car to rush through a red light just like the human driven cars. If not, the human driven cars are going to potentially ram into the back of a self-driving car that opts to come to a legally proper stop but that is a kilter to the customs and norms of the drivers in that country.

For parking purposes, especially in Japanese major cities, there are often parking towers that require a car to be driven onto a waiting pan, which then rotates upward and brings down a next empty pan. Imagine this is like a kind of Ferris wheel, but used to park cars. You can therefore in tight city space park more cars by having them parked up on a tower. A Level 5 self-driving car should have AI that allows it to properly park on such towers, and also be able to resume motion once the self-driving car is released from the parking tower.

There is a tendency in some areas of Japan to have cars decide to stop at the edge of a road, blocking traffic. Human drivers do this all the time. The AI needs to ascertain what is taking place and avoid hitting the stopped car. One might also ask whether the AI should abide by that same custom. In other words, should the AI go ahead and be willing to stop at the edge of the road and potentially block oncoming traffic?

Some of the software developers that are doing the AI for self-driving cars are telling me that they won't let the self-driving car do anything that seems either illegal or dangerous in terms of driving of the car. But, if the custom in a country is that there is a standard practice of stopping a car to let passengers in or out, or wait for someone, shouldn't that still be provided by the self-driving car?

This brings us to an important element of consideration about self-driving cars. Should the self-driving car decide what is proper or not proper in terms of driving practices and then permeate that across the globe? The at-times subset of "righteous" developers of the AI for self-driving cars would say yes. They would say that it is wrong for a self-driving car to rush a red light at an intersection, or to park at the side of the road and become a roadway hazard to other cars. They therefore are refusing to allow the AI to do such things.

Here's another one that gets them rankled. In some countries, the hitting of small animals such as squirrels or even cats is widely accepted if those animals veer onto the roadway and become a roadway obstacle. There are developers here in the United States that find this driving behavior abhorrent and so they are insisting that the self-driving car would need to take whatever evasive maneuvers it could to ensure that it didn't hit a squirrel or a cat. But, if this AI then endangers the human occupants or actually causes injury to the occupants in the self-driving car, one would need to question whether the avoidance of hitting the small animal was "right" or not. In that country, and in its customs, it would have been well accepted to hit the animal, even though in say the United States it might be considered abhorrent.

For a Level 5 self-driving car, the automation and AI is supposed to be able to drive the car in whatever manner that a human driver could have driven the car. The question then arises, what about internationalizing of that crucial principle? Does this mean that if a human driver in country X drives in a certain manner Y, and yet that manner Y is contrary in some fashion to driving manner Z, and that driving manner Z is acceptable in certain countries, what should the self-driving car be able and made to do?

Our view so far is that a self-driving car should do as the locals do.

We are developing AI that embodies the customs and practices of specific countries and therefore will drive like a local drivers. The AI needs to be aware of the differences in laws and regulations, the differences in language, the differences in the driving environment (such as roadways, highways, etc.), and also the differences in how people in that country actually drive (their customs and everyday practices).

I know that some dreamers say that once we have all self-driving cars and no more human-driven cars that then we can have a homogeneous driving practice across the entire globe. That day is far, far, far, far away into the future. For now, we need to figure out how to have self-driving cars that mix with human driven cars. You've probably seen Western drivers that try to drive in a foreign country and seen how the other human drivers there will berate the westerner for not abiding by local customs in driving. We are aiming to have self-driving cars that blend into the driving practices of the local international location. Self-driving cars need to earn their international driver's license and be able to drive like a local.

Our motto for self-driving cars is "do as the locals do, within reason, and be flexible about it."

CHAPTER 16
SLEEPING AS AI MECHANISM FOR SELF-DRIVING CARS

CHAPTER 16
SLEEPING AS AI MECHANISM FOR SELF-DRIVING CARS

How long can you go without sleep?

We've all done an all-nighter when studying for a final exam. As a software developer, you've likely gone several seemingly sleepless nights while trying to hit that all-important deadline for getting the software done and out the door. For most people, going for about three days without sleep is as far as they can go. Some years ago, radio stations and even TV shows had contests to see who could avoid going to sleep the longest. In some instances, there were situations such as having to stand and put your palm on a car, and whomever lasted the longest would win the car. These tests of human endurance about sleep were gradually either outlawed or were considered of such poor taste that they are rarely if ever done these days.

In 1965, there is the famous case of a 17-year-old student in high school that sought to make a new record for the longest officially recognized time without sleep. During a science fair, he managed to avoid sleep for about 11 days (a recorded 264 hours). Researchers have done similar kinds of studies and found that some can avoid sleep for around 8 to 10 days, but this is not the usual case. Furthermore, as you might guess, the subjects began to get quite irritable and difficult to deal with.

You likely know people at work that seem to get insufficient sleep and tend to exhibit various cognitive deficits or dysfunctions. Most commonly there is a gradual reduction in ability to concentrate and the mind of the sleepless person begins to wander. Motivation usually drops and the person becomes confused about what they were doing and why there were doing it. All in all, there is a definite and apparent degradation in mental processing and especially at the higher-levels of abstract reasoning and thinking.

Motor functions of the human body can also be impacted by a lack of sleep. There have been cases of drivers that got so drowsy that they reported they weren't able to move their feet onto the brake fast enough to avoid an accident, one that they would normally have been able to avoid if they had been more fully alert. Sensory perception is often impacted by sleeplessness. People that have been deprived of sleep will sometimes hear sounds that aren't there, or see images that aren't there, and otherwise be unable to accurately make use of their normal sensory capabilities. There have been cases of drivers that swore they saw an animal dart in front of their car and so they swerved and got into an accident, when in fact there was no indication at all that an animal had been there and it was instead attributed to lack of sleep that the driver reported.

You can try to fight going to sleep, but the body and mind seem to inexorably force you into a state of sleeping. As the famous saying goes, you can delay sleep, but you cannot defeat it. Experiments with rats showed that by going without sleep for two weeks, the rats actually died. The experimenters kept forcing the rats to stay awake and eventually they collapsed entirely and died. There is debate about whether the sleeplessness actually caused the death, and so we won't here deal with that acrimonious debate. The main point is that it seems like humans and indeed apparently all animals appear to need sleep.

When you think about the nature of sleep, you realize how dangerous a thing it is. While you or any animal is asleep, it is at a heightened risk of survival. You aren't fully aware of your surroundings. You are subject to someone or something sneaking up upon you. That someone or something could readily harm you, capture you, or kill you. Many animals undertake elaborate protections when they sleep, such as burrowing into the ground or finding a secluded spot in a cave or at the top of a tree. As humans, we often close and lock the door to our bedrooms and sleep in a room that is generally a protective bubble, aiming to make sure that we aren't readily subject to our sleeping state vulnerability.

Why would humans and animals generally have evolved in such a manner that we needed sleep, which as pointed out is a significant danger to survival. One would certainly think that over time the evolutionary forces would have led to us not needing sleep, doing so by "out surviving" those that do need sleep. Yet, sleep still persists. There must be a really, really, really good reason for sleep.

No one can say for sure why we do need sleep.

One argument is that we need sleep to give the body a chance to recover and recuperate. After a long day of effort, presumably the body is worn out. Therefore, it would seem to make sense to force the body into a state of motionless so that it could work toward fixing itself and getting ready for the next day's efforts. If this were the case, you might ask why couldn't we just rest. In other words, rather than entering into actual sleep, suppose we just let our body rest for a couple of hours each night. Wouldn't that take care of the whole my-body-needs-recovery aspects?

The counter-argument is that maybe people and animals would not be careful enough to let their body rest, and so this sleep mechanism came to the forefront to force us to let our bodies rest. With the mind also going into a sleep mode, it would then force the body to have resting time. Were the mind to continue to remain active, it might overtax the body and keep the body going all the time, ultimately destroying the body. If the body gets destroyed, the mind has no place to go. Thus, the mind must enter into sleep, whether it wants to or not, in order to keep the body going by allowing the body to rest, and for which then the mind still has a means to function because the body is kept in good shape.

That's a theory that most don't buy into. Instead, the belief is that the mind also needs sleep. In fact, there are some camps that say that it is really only the mind that needs sleep. They assert that the body could be kept going all the time. The mind is the weak link in all of this sleep stuff. If you could keep the mind from going to sleep, the body could rest enough at times to keep going all of the time. The only reason the body goes to sleep is due to the mind going to sleep. When the mind sleeps, the body has nothing to control it, and so the body just naturally also goes into a motionless state.

I am sure that you know though that the mind does not seem to truly go to sleep. There used to be a belief that the mind went entirely dormant during sleep. The neurons and brain activity were assumed to stop. We know now that this is not the case. There is activity in the brain during sleep. Indeed, you might be aware of REM (Rapid Eye Movement), a sleep phase found in at least mammals and birds, involving rapid eye movements, low muscle movements, and the likelihood of dreams occurring.

Do animals dream? Researchers have tried to show that it seems that they do, including studies of birds that suggested they were dreaming while asleep. People often say that they dreamed last night and are sure that they dreamed, but they cannot remember the dream per se. They also will claim that it was their first dream in weeks. Generally, this is likely a false recollection. You normally are dreaming whenever you sleep. It is only that some of those dreams do you ever seem to become aware of, after having come out of sleep. There is also the chance that you believe you dreamed but in fact it is entirely made-up. You believe that dreams can be remembered and so you convince yourself that you had a dream and you claim you can remember it, when maybe you didn't at all.

People and animals that go without sleep for a while are prone to cognitive deficits and dysfunctions. We might therefore use this as a clue about the nature of sleep. Why would we for example hallucinate once we've been deprived of sleep? What is going on during sleep in the mind that without sleep the mind turns toward hallucinations?

A prevailing theory about the mind during sleep is that it is reorganizing itself. Pretend for a moment that you are working in an office that has lots of filing cabinets. During the day, your in-box gets filled up, and you try to process things and move them into your out-box. Meanwhile, you are also filing the paperwork into the cabinets. You want the paperwork to be ordered in some helpful way, and perhaps you've opted to label the cabinets by the alphabet. You place some of your files into the cabinets marked A to D, and later on, when you need to find that paperwork, you'll know to look in the A-D labeled cabinet to find it.

Some believe that the human brain works the same way. During wakefulness, your brain is trying to process all of the sensory input coming into the in-box, and producing output via the out-box, such as speaking or waving your arms or whatever. The brain is also filing memories as fast as it can, while you are awake. Maybe, the brain can only do so much while also needing to pay attention to the world. Perhaps, it needs some dedicated downtime to be able to properly organize memories and file them into the right places.

One reason why this theory seems plausible is that when you have dreams, it could be that a dream is really a snapshot of the filing that is going on. Things are kind of in a mess during the filing process, and the dream inadvertently arises from that mess. This explains why dreams often involve aspects that are seemingly unrelated. They were merely crisscrossing throughout the brain as they were being filed. This also explains why there is activity in the brain during sleep. It is doing (in parlance of software) garbage collection. Some stuff in the brain is being filed, some stuff is being discarded (maybe), some stuff is being transformed, some stuff is being packed or compacted, and so on.

Another fitting piece of the puzzle involves the mind gradually become cognitively dysfunctional when denied sleep. Using the garbage collection theory, we could suppose that the brain in a waking state eventually reaches a threshold that the amount of input has piled up so much that the brain can no longer properly function. It's like an office that begins to have piles upon piles of files all over the floor and sitting on shelves. Until it all gets labeled and placed neatly into the filing cabinets, it becomes harder to use and begins to get jumbled together. Our hallucinations are a combination of the mental input spilling over and getting mixed with our normal conscious selves. The mind gets full of "garbage" that needs to be organized and transformed, but since it is being denied filing time (sleep), it does what it can in real-time to keep processing in spite of the junk mixing into everything.

After being denied sleep for an extended time, by-and-large most humans are able to return back to a normal mental state after getting so-called catch-up sleep. This again fits well with the garbage collection theory. Presumably, once the mind gets a chance to sleep, it then continues the garbage collection. It could be that the piled up trash in the mind takes an extra amount of sleep time to properly organize and get setup for normal mental processing.

A recent study on sleep found that even upside-down jellyfish sleep. This was unexpected, since they do not have a brain per se. Jellyfish make use of a decentralized network of nerve cells. Biologists say that this is the first time that an animal without a centralized nervous system has been shown to actually sleep. If the Cassiopea jellyfish really do sleep, and since they evolved from a lineage going back around 542 million years, it once again suggests that sleep is a very long time needed factor. You might wonder though that if sleep is due to the mind needing time off, do jellyfish really need time off to let their decentralized nerve cells do something? Some experts are puzzled by this and more research needs to be done.

What does this all have to do with self-driving cars?

At the Cybernetic Self-Driving Car Institute, we are making use of sleep as an AI mechanism for self-driving cars. This is a novel idea and few others are pursuing this. We explain next our rationale for why we think this has merit.

First, let's focus on an overall argument about the nature of AI and how we will ultimately achieve AI. Some believe that the only path to true AI involves being able to ultimately mimic human intelligence. Since human intelligence appears to depend on sleep, we would presumably need to crack the code on why sleep is needed, and then either have systems that do something like sleep or actually really go to sleep in the same manner of the human mind.

Thus, if you are pursuing AI, you should also be wanting to pursue the nature of the human mind and how it works, and also therefore what sleep does and why it is seemingly so important to the human mind and presumably to the ability to think.

I'll note that there are some AI researchers that believe we don't need to know how the human mind works in order to achieve intelligence in machines. They say that there is more than one way to skin a cat. For them, if you can get a machine to exhibit the same characteristics as a human intelligence, then how you got there is immaterial to the matter at hand. Others say that those trying to find other means to get to intelligence are barking up a false tree and ought to get back to figuring out how human intelligence actually works.

Anyway, let's go ahead and assume that there is a need for sleep in cognition, and therefore there might be a basis for having sleep occur in AI.

In the case of a self-driving car, what does this translate into? One perspective is that the AI of the self-driving car needs downtime to be able to process all of the inputs and processing and memories that were collected during its wakefulness state. This is in keeping with the earlier mentioned theory about the purpose of sleep in humans is for software related garbage collection. When a self-driving car is not otherwise in motion and functioning as a working car, we can use the downtime for the self-driving car to do a similar kind of systems related garbage collection.

This though admittedly is not an entirely satisfying answer, since you could presumably just add more processors and even offload processing to a remote centralized server, which then could enable the garbage collection while the self-driving car is still in an operating mode and not require actual downtime of the self-driving car.

Speaking of which, there is ongoing debate about whether or not self-driving cars are going to be operating 24×7. Your existing car tends to be "asleep" while you are not using it, meaning that it is at rest. Right now, there aren't any smarts per se on your conventional car, so you could suggest that the body of the car is resting. In one way, though this might seem odd, it does kind of make sense in that suppose your car was operating continuously 24×7. How much could your car engine take? Is it really made to be continuously operating?

For those that are thinking that they are going to turn their self-driving car into a 24×7 ride sharing service, meaning that while the owner is not using the self-driving car that it will be driving around earning money by giving rides, we need to consider how realistic this will be. Cars are not particularly made in such a manner that it is expected they will continually be in operation. I am not saying they cannot operate continuously. I am just saying we are going to see a different pattern of when and how cars breakdown and need repairs, in comparison to how cars are operated and used today.

Getting back to the parallels between sleep in humans and the potential need for sleep in AI, there is the point already made about the role of garbage collection. For our self-driving car software, we are making use of the processors of the self-driving car when it is not being used (the self-driving car is parked, not in motion, not tasked with any direct activity; it might or might not be that the car is turned-off), essentially mimicking the sleep notion, and having the system review what it has most recently learned. This allows the self-driving car to create new approaches to driving and put into fast indexing lessons learned. During the normal driving of the self-driving car, the AI is busy with driving the car, and so this downtime can be put to handy use.

We also believe that there are more mental aspects underlying sleep than what is known or theorized currently. Using large-scale neural networks, we are simulating various hypotheses about other facets of sleep.

We are exercising processing changes across the neural network to simulate sleeping like states, in terms of potentially serving to tune the mind. This is more than just filing of memories.

For self-driving cars, whether you believe that they should "sleep" or not, we can at least be spurred by the concept of sleep to leverage when the physical body (the car) is not being used. This is an opportunity to leverage the then under-utilized AI that is presumably otherwise dormant when the car is not actively engaged in motion and driving.

NEW ADVANCES IN AI AUTONOMOUS DRIVERLESS SELF-DRIVING CARS

I hope that our efforts will spur others to give due consideration to why sleep is crucial to humans and cognition, and in what ways might that be applied to AI and self-driving cars. I ask that you sleep on it..

CHAPTER 17
CAR INSURANCE SCAMS AND SELF-DRIVING CARS

CHAPTER 17

CAR INSURANCE SCAMS AND SELF-DRIVING CARS

I drive a somewhat exotic luxury car. Driving around, I am at times especially aware of the fact that it is a pricey car and either get accolades from other drivers and pedestrians, or at times receive ire from those that think it is wrong to drive such a car (ecologically because it is a gas guzzler, or because it seems boastful and a brag). Some places that I drive are equally filled with such exotic cars, and sometimes even more elaborate ones. In other cases, I drive in areas where the car stands out because the other cars in the area tend to be less expensive. In those areas, it instantly draws attention.

Some drivers of such exotic cars relish the attention, wherever and whenever they drive. For me, I am not that keen on the attention, especially in places that seem suspect. When I park the car on the streets in downtown Los Angeles, I never know whether when I come back if the car will be still there (might be stolen), or might be marred (graffiti or worse). One of my previous cars had actually got stolen (I am a statistic now).

Driving this kind of a car has other potential consequences too.

The other day, I was on the freeway and driving along without incident. Suddenly, a rather ragged car came up from behind me, switched into the lane to my left, zipped ahead, and then opted to unexpectedly jump into my lane directly in front of me. There didn't seem to be any obvious reason for this driving behavior. If the driver was trying to get ahead in traffic, the act of getting into my lane at that moment actually slowed down the progress of the other driver. Given the seemingly frantic movements, the driver should have stayed in the lane it had gotten into, or upon getting into my lane the driver should have accelerated further forward since there was empty space ahead.

As Spiderman might say, my spidey sense was tingling. Things weren't adding up.

I next saw another ragged car coming up behind me, and it suddenly switched into the lane to my left. As it drove past me, I gave the driver a hard look. The driver seemed to be acting like they didn't see me, but I am sure they must have. The driver was focused straight ahead. I noticed though that the driver ahead of me seemed to be studying his rearview mirror. For whatever reason, he suddenly seemed quite interested in what was happening behind him.

If I had not been paying attention, I would have just continued forward and not given much thought to what was occurring around me. Nothing explicit had yet happened. A car was ahead of me, and a car was to my left. They were both driving quickly, faster than the surrounding cars. They were both cars of a bit ragged in nature. They were presumably completely independent of each other. But, I just felt that maybe they were somehow connected to each other.

I opted to switch over to the rightmost lane. There was no real need to do so, but it seemed like it might be handy to change lanes and see what else would happen with the other two cars. The car that had been ahead of me tried to follow me over to the rightmost lane. He was blocked though by other cars. The cars in my lane then passed him. Meanwhile, the other car that had been to my left opted to slow down and keep pace with the other car. Why didn't that driver zoom forward, which seemed like what he was earlier trying to accomplish?

The whole situation smelled. I knew that an upcoming freeway exit could be used to get off the freeway and just a block afterward would be an entrance that I could use to get back onto the freeway. At the last possible moment, I veered into the exit and got off the freeway. When I then drove ahead and got back onto the freeway, the other two cars were no longer to be seen (assuming they continued at the speed of the freeway, they would have been a distance ahead by then).

I might have just avoided a swoop and squat.

Are you familiar with a swoop and squat? If not, welcome to the vocabulary known to those that deal with car insurance fraud. The swoop and squat is the name given to a series of maneuvers by criminals trying to force a car accident.

Here's how it works. Two vehicles (or more) work together to execute the swoop and squat. A driver in a lead car (the squatter) will get ahead of a target car. The target car is usually an expensive vehicle, which has been identified while driving along as a good candidate to be involved in an insurance fraud. The second criminal car moves ahead of the now lead criminal car and the target car. The front most criminal car then swoops into the front of the squatter. The squatter jams on their brakes. The target car driver then also presumably tries to quickly brake, but with the short distance between them and the squatter, they are going to rear-end the squatter car.

The swoop car then darts away and does not stop for the accident that it has now apparently caused. Meanwhile, the squatter car and the target car usually agree to stop and exchange insurance information. The squatter car might even have more than just the driver in it, perhaps several occupants. This allows the squatter car to potentially make multiple insurance claims, including that the occupants of the squatter car claim various injuries.

The beauty of this "accident" will be that the target car driver is usually held responsible for hitting the squatter car. You can of course try to profess that there was another car that cut-off the squatter car and that the squatter car messed-up. But, you would be held accountable for not allowing sufficient driving distance between you and the car ahead of you. It's a mess. The scammers have staged the whole thing, and any savvy insurance adjuster is going to recognize it. Unfortunately, the odds are that the scammers will probably get away with the scam.

You might be thinking that this kind of scamming rarely occurs.

You'd be wrong! I am either proud or disappointed to let you know that Los Angeles is considered the capital of auto insurance fraud. The California Department of Insurance (CDI) has about one hundred detectives devoted to auto insurance fraud. They are widely overworked and undermanned for the volume of auto insurance fraud occurring. Some of the auto insurance fraud is well organized and accomplished by gangs or other criminal enterprises.

The payoff can be high for those that commit auto insurance fraud. Insurance companies have deep pockets. They need to weigh the payout versus the effort to prove some kind of auto insurance fraud. Los Angeles is attractive to scammers because it has a goodly percentage of high-value vehicles, it has a tremendous amount of daily traffic, and lots of non-scam accidents that happen all the time. Thus, the scam car accidents are easier to pull off and can more readily hide among the many other non-scam car accidents that occur. If you were a criminal and tried to pull the scam in some other locale, it might be more suspicious and standout to police and the insurance companies.

The scammers will try to make as much money of a scam as they can. They will often take their damaged squatter car to an auto-body shop that is also involved in the scam. The car body shop will make the damage appear to be more extensive than it really was. Either they will file false indications about the damage, or in some instances they will even do more damage to the car to make sure that it really does appear to have the extensive damage claimed. The occupants of the squatter car will potentially claim personal injuries due to the accident. They might have a physician that's also involved in the fraud ring. The physician will substantiate the false injuries and then get a part of the loot for the scam.

If convicted, the scammers could face some serious prison time since this kind of fraud is considered a felony. They could also be financially penalized too. In one sense, this though is a type of fraud that is one of the least likely to be spotted. It is a low likelihood that it will be investigated. It is a low likelihood that it will be prosecuted.

Sadly, the amount of money to be made by the scam, versus the chances of getting caught and getting penalized, means that auto insurance fraud continues to be a budding business.

Was I faced with a potential swoop and squat when I was on the freeway? I don't know for sure. It certainly had the right ingredients. I was driving a high-value car. I was on a crowded freeway. The potential squat car had purposely maneuvered in front of me, when there didn't seem to be any reasonable reason to do so. It was a ragged car. The second car, the potential swoop car, appeared to be working in conjunction with the other car. It was a ragged car. They were both positioning themselves into a classic swoop and squat situation. It might have been only in my mind, but I figured it was worth taking a mild evasive action to avoid the chances of getting mired in an auto insurance fraud case.

What does this have to do with self-driving cars?

At the Cybernetic Self-Driving Car Institute, we are developing AI for self-driving cars that detects these kinds of potential auto insurance fraud scam maneuvers and then seeks to avoid getting mired in them.

When I give presentations about our work at autonomous vehicle conferences, one of the first objections that I get is that there will not be a need for detecting auto insurance fraud cases, which purportedly is because once we have all self-driving cars on the roads there will no longer be any such scams. In other words, if we have all self-driving cars on the road, these self-driving cars would not act in such a nefarious manner. In this nirvana world, all self-driving cars are respectful of each other and we won't have scam accidents.

Wake-up! We are going to have a mixture of human driven cars and self-driving cars for many, many, many years to come. This idea that by some magic act that suddenly all of the human driven cars disappear and are entirely replaced by self-driving cars is not realistic. It is a crazy dream. Therefore, self-driving cars must be prepared to interact with and deal with human driven cars. Period.

I would also like to add an aside. These same dreamers think that self-driving cars will always be respectful of the laws of driving and that they will always be respectful to other self-driving cars. Why will this be the case? It assumes again some kind of idealized world. We can pretty much anticipate that self-driving cars are going to be varying from this all-respect approach. We might even see scammers that hack a self-driving car to participate in scams. There are likely even going to be new kinds of scams involving self-driving cars that we aren't even thinking about as yet (some self-driving cars will be targets, some will be perpetrators).

Another question that I sometimes get involves the aspect of whether self-driving cars will have car insurance. Normally, the driver of the car is the one that has the auto insurance. But, if the driver is AI, who then has the car insurance? Will the AI have the car insurance?

We pretty much can reject the notion that AI will be considered the equivalent of a human and be getting car insurance. The auto maker that made the self-driving car might be the one that has the auto insurance for the car, or someone else such as the tech firm that made the AI, or others. I think we can all agree that one way or another, self-driving cars are going to have car insurance. I don't think we're going to have uninsured self-driving cars driving around on our public roadways (well, at least not legally doing so).

When self-driving cars first get mired in auto insurance scams, it will be a highly visible issue. The scammers will probably try to claim that the AI was mistaken and that it caused the accident. This though is something that today's scammers are generally not sophisticated enough to try and pull off. Plus, it would make them overly visible. Nonetheless, I am sure that self-driving cars will be an attractive target. These first self-driving cars will be high-value cars and probably have high-value occupants.

In fact, you could suggest that self-driving cars are going to be ripe and easy targets. Most self-driving cars today are being developed without the kinds of defensive driving tactics that human drivers know and use. Self-driving cars tend to act like a novice driver. They are easy to fool. You might be aware of the famous case of the self-driving car that came to a four-way stop. The other human driven cars were able to roll through the stop signs and the self-driving car kept waiting its turn. In a similar manner, I am sure that scammers will be aware of the limitations of the self-driving cars in the marketplace and be able to exploit those limitations to undertake an auto insurance scam.

Another form of today's auto insurance frauds involves bicycle riders that intentionally ram into a car. These bike riders are willing to get hit by a car, in order to file an insurance claim. Usually, though, these scams are dealt with immediately in that the bike rider asks the human driver for cash to make the case go away. Asking for say $200 cash is an easy scam and the driver will often want to avoid the insurance paperwork, so they give the cash to the scammer and continue along on their driving journey.

Anyway, let's get back to the AI of self-driving cars and how it needs to be prepared to cope with potential auto insurance scams.

We are developing and testing AI that recognizes the swoop and squat. Similar to how I noticed the actions of other cars around me, there is a module in the AI of a self-driving car that is watching for signs of a potential scam. In the case of the swoop and squat, it sits aside of the rest of the AI driving the car, and tries to see if there is something suspicious about the other cars around the self-driving car. If it spots something potentially amiss, it notifies the strategic and tactical AI components that are driving the car. If the suspicion has a high enough probability, and if an avoidance effort can be done without undue risk, the self-driving car will take appropriate evasive action.

The self-driving car can also let the occupants know about what has taken place. The human occupants in the self-driving car might wonder why the self-driving car has suddenly exited from the freeway and then decided to enter back onto the freeway. There is an explanation system that can communicate to the occupants what has occurred. In some case, the occupants might not want to know and not care, while in other instances the occupants might be keenly interested to know.

Besides the swoop and squat, we also have the AI system be on the watch for other kinds of auto insurance scams.

There is the panic stop scam, consisting of just one squatter and no swoop car.

There is the start and stop, again usually done with one criminal driven car ahead of you.

There's the wave-in, in which the human driver seems to offer you an opening in their lane and then rams into your car. This is harder for a conventional self-driving car to get caught up in, due to the aspect that the human driver of the criminal car usually makes a hand signal to the human driver of the target car. But, it still can be done with a self-driving car by making a tempting opening for the self-driving car and then ramming into it when it takes the opening.

Another scam is the sideswipe. This involves intersections that have two left turns. The criminal car will swerve into the lane of the target car.

It is hard to know in-advance that a scam is going to occur. The actions of the scammers can be similarly done innocently by regular drivers that are careless. Thus, there is no clear-cut way to know that a scam is being setup. That being said, whether a scam or not, the risk factor of getting involved in an accident is certainly detectable in all of these maneuvers. A good self-driving car should have a robust defensive driving AI capability to be watchful of these potential situations. These particular maneuvers such as the swoop and squat should even more so be on the defensive watch, since they are being done by both regular drivers and the scamming drivers.

It will be interesting to see how scammers find ways to especially make use of self-driving cars in their nefarious efforts. Besides the type of driving scams that I've mentioned, there are other scams such as staged auto thefts, there are dumped vehicle frauds (scammers dump a car into a lake and claim it was stolen), there are born again vehicles (a stolen vehicle is given a new Vehicle Identification Number or VIN, and used in a scam), and so on.

NEW ADVANCES IN AI AUTONOMOUS DRIVERLESS SELF-DRIVING CARS

I know that many are hoping that self-driving cars are going to improve the world as we know it. There are indeed many ways in which self-driving cars are going to aid us. At the same time, without seeming to be pessimistic, I am sure that we will see criminal minds trying to find ways to involve self-driving cars into criminal acts. Let's try to make the AI for self-driving cars good enough that self-driving cars won't be ready unknowing dupes or accomplices in the rotten work of criminals.

CHAPTER 18
U-TURN TRAVERSAL AI FOR SELF-DRIVING CARS

CHAPTER 18
U-TURN TRAVERSAL AI
FOR SELF-DRIVING CARS

It seems that the U-turn maneuver makes drivers do crazy things.

As an example, the other day I was driving northbound on Pacific Coast Highway (PCH). There is a stretch of this highway that for several miles you are pretty much forced to continue in a straight line because there aren't any viable turn-offs. There are some spots that allow you to enter into a beach parking lot, but otherwise once you've decided to get onto PCH at one end of the stretch and assuming you are trying to get to the other end of the stretch, you are at the mercy of whatever might happen on that stretch of road.

Well, the other day the northbound traffic got snarled due to an accident at the far northern end of the stretch. This meant that hundreds of cars heading northbound were now sitting on PCH as though it was a parking lot. We were all waiting for that accident up ahead to get cleared and allow traffic to continue forward. You could see the look of exasperation and worse on the faces of the drivers that were wanting to get to work, or get their kids to school, or proceed to whatever seemingly urgent destination and not desirous of sitting around for the many minutes waiting for the stretch to open up.

Other than getting onto one's cell phone to make calls or maybe changing radio stations to listen to the news or perhaps soothing music, there wasn't anything else that could be done. Or so it seemed. Instead of waiting it out, cars began to decide they would make a U-turn and head southbound. Going southbound at this juncture was kind of questionable because you'd need to go all the way back to the initial entry point of this stretch, and then find some other means of navigating byzantine roads to eventually end-up toward the northbound side of the highway. Doing so would certainly add at least as much time that you would incur by just waiting for this northbound stretch to clear. But, for those especially that have little patience, I guess they decided they'd rather be in motion, even if it meant that it might be longer to get to their destination, than to sit still.

This stretch of PCH had a few left turn spots that were intended to get you into a beach parking lot. Cars stuck in the stretch that were near to the left turns then proceeded to pretend they were going to make a left turn and then actually made a U-turn. Only one problem was that there were signs posted at each of these left turns that said "No U-turn" (which, unless I misunderstand such signs, means, you can't make a U-turn there!). Furthermore, other cars that weren't near to a left turn spot were deciding to make a U-turn from whatever place they were, doing so across a doubled set of double yellow lines (which, in California means that you aren't supposed to cross it, this is considered an uncrossable median generally).

I am sure you might be sympathetic to these drivers that were making all of these illegal U-turns and be thinking that it seemed like the right thing to do, since they were being blocked from going northbound and so why not just turn around and head the other way. This might be sensible except for the fact that the southbound traffic was moving at quite a pace, and thus these northbound turnarounds were not only impeding the southbound traffic, it was causing near collisions and making havoc out of the southbound lanes. These thoughtless U-turn drivers were risking the lives of the southbound traffic drivers. And, it was forcing those southbound traffic drivers to swerve and brake so much that I anticipated we'd see some of them inadvertently go across the doubled set of double yellow lines and plow directly into the now sitting ducks drivers on the northbound side. It was an ugly situation for sure.

In my experience, it seems as though many drivers rely upon making a U-turn whenever they feel like it is okay to do so, and often ignore whether the U-turn is illegal to make. A novice driver is taught the rules-of-the-road that they are not supposed to make a U-turn when it is unsafe to do so. They are told that in a residential district they cannot make a U-turn when vehicles are approaching within 200 feet of your car. They are told you cannot make a U-turn when there is a "No U-turn" sign posted. They are informed that you are not to make a U-turn at a railroad crossing – which, by the way, I end up weekly at a railroad crossing on my morning commute and I see at least one or two cars that make a U-turn once they see that the arms have come down to block the street for the train.

My point is that in spite of what we are supposed to do, and what we are not supposed to do, human drivers often decide what they want to do and act without necessarily considering the legal aspects and nor the safety aspects of making a U-turn.

What does this have to do with self-driving cars?

At the Cybernetic Self-Driving Car Institute, we are developing AI software for self-driving cars that deal with U-turns in the following two key ways:

(1) Be aware of what other drivers might do when a situation presents itself such that they might make some form of radical U-turn and therefore the AI of the self-driving car should be predicting and planning for such haphazard driving by other drivers,

(2) Be able to execute a U-turn as a self-driving car when it is so needed and appropriate to do so.

In the case of the first aspect, being on the watch for U-turns, if a self-driving car were going southbound on PCH the day that I was on that stretch, the AI should have been noticing the long line of traffic northbound and could have reasonably predicted that there might be ad hoc U-turns by some of those cars. This would require the knowledge that the stretch was a pipeline with little other chance of getting out of it, and that the time of day was such that car drivers are often especially in a semi-panic driving mode.

The self-driving car would also have been able to see up ahead of it that some cars were trying to make a U-turn into the southbound traffic. By use of the self-driving car sensors, such as LIDAR, radar, and the cameras, it would have seen or detected that cars were making these illegal U-turns. As such, the self-driving car should be making defensive maneuvers to anticipate those U-turn drivers that were wreaking havoc with southbound traffic.

I realize that some of you might say that there wasn't need for the self-driving car to have to "understand" what was happening and that it could have merely just reacted to the road conditions of having cars coming into the southbound lanes. I contend though that if the self-driving car is only reacting to the straight-ahead traffic, it is not going to do as safe a job as it can in terms of preparing for and avoiding potential collisions with those other U-turn making cars.

Which would you prefer to have, a self-driving car that drives like someone that has blinders and can only see what is straight ahead of it, or one that is surveying the scene and grasps the bigger picture of what traffic is doing? I would much prefer the more sophisticated self-driving car that drives like real human drivers do (at least for the "good" aspects of human driving). Most human drivers would have noticed that the northbound lanes were packed and have easily predicted that there would be crazy U-turns. It's a natural aspect for anyone that has driven for any length of time.

Besides being able to predict and deal with U-turns made by others, we also of course want a self-driving car to be able to make a U-turn (that's the second major aspect of self-driving cars and U-turns, namely, the self-driving car being able to safely execute a U-turn).

There are some that believe that a self-driving car should only make a U-turn at a controlled intersection that has a green left turn light and that's the only time that a U-turn should be made by a self-driving car. In essence, they don't want self-driving cars to make other kinds of legal U-turns that are less controlled by the roadway circumstances. They view that U-turns are so risky that only when a self-driving car is forced into making a fully legal and tightly controlled situation U-turn that it would then embark upon a U-turn.

For us, we think this is a rather myopic view and that a U-turn should be part and parcel as an essential driving tool of a self-driving car. The notion that a U-turn is just too dangerous and that the self-driving car should not know how to do it per se, in the sense of knowing in varying kinds of situations, limits what a self-driving car can do. If we want to achieve true Level 5 self-driving cars, which are ones that can drive in any circumstance that a human driver could drive a car, we must have the AI be able to deal with U-turns in the same variety of situations that a human driver could legally do a U-turn.

I'll also put a bit of a qualifier around the word "legally" doing a U-turn. Going back to the PCH situation, you could certainly say that the drivers making the U-turns were doing so illegally.

On other hand, there is a provision in the state driving laws that allows for making otherwise illegal maneuvers in situations that doing so are dire or special. Suppose that a police officer was directing traffic and was telling drivers to make a U-turn that otherwise was illegal to do, it presumably at that moment would be a legal U-turn because you were acting at the direction of the police officer.

The point being that sometimes an illegal driving act can be considered a legal one, and thus the self-driving car cannot just blindly assume that if a driving maneuver is normally considered illegal that it is always wrong to invoke it.

In quick recap, those that say never have a self-driving car do a U-turn are wrong to say this, since there are circumstances that making a legal U-turn are allowed and also some circumstances where making a U-turn is actually required (such as the police officer directing cars to make a U-turn). Self-driving cars need to know how to make U-turns. Period. They also need to know how other drivers make U-turns and therefore be better prepared as a defensive driver.

Speaking of being a defensive driver that knows about U-turns, here are some of the contextual situation of U-turns that we are having the AI be aware of:

U-turn Mania

These are situations where en masse there are drivers that are going to be trying to make U-turns. Typical scenario involves cars that are stuck in a traffic situation such as my example earlier on PCH. This can happen on a highway, a freeway, and even occurs in parking lots such as when I attend Dodge baseball games and as the drivers all try to leave the stadium parking lot at the same time they then resort to making wild U-turns en masse in hopes of finding a faster exit elsewhere.

U-turn Panic

These are situations involving a driver that suddenly realizes they are heading the wrong direction and so they panic and try to make a U-turn erratically, regardless of how safe or wise it is to make the U-turn. You've likely seen these kinds of drivers. They will often dart across several lanes of traffic to get to a left turn lane and then make their U-turn. When they execute the U-turn, it is often done recklessly.

U-turn Clod

These are situations involving someone that is making a U-turn and has not calculated properly how to do so in the circumstance. They start the U-turn, then realize they cannot make it in one smooth move, get caught by the narrow width of the road, and then switch into a 3-point turn mode of stopping, backing up, and then completing the U-turn. Very dangerous.

U-turn Frozen

This is the situation of someone that has gotten into a posture to likely make a U-turn, but it might appear to be a left-turn, and even though they could have made a left turn, they realize that the traffic is such that they cannot yet make a U-turn, so they sit in the left turn lane and keep waiting until the traffic allows for a U-turn. Cars behind them in the left turn lane are upset that the dolt seems to not be making a left turn. They don't necessarily realize that the person is wanting to make a U-turn and waiting until it is safe to do so. They sit seemingly frozen.

As might be apparent from the above, the AI of the self-driving car is watching for these situations and making sure it is defensively ready to handle these situations. It is feasible for example to calculate that a U-turn Clod is possibly going to happen, since the self-driving car can ascertain whether a car that appears to be wanting to make a U-turn can actually make the U-turn in one move or not. If it appears unlikely that it can be done in one move, the self-driving car will slow down and possibly even come to a halt upon the start of the execution of the U-turn by the other car.

This also brings up another aspect about car drivers and U-turns. A human driver that is desirous of making a U-turn is often gauging whether oncoming traffic is going to allow the U-turn or not. If the oncoming traffic is aggressive then the U-turn driver will often wait to make the U-turn. Human drivers will assess the other cars and their drivers, and if it seems like other drivers are "sheep" in their view, they will make the U-turn and assume that those other drivers will let them do so. On the other hand, if the other drivers are aggressive and unlikely to back down, the U-turn driver will realize they have to wait. It's a game of chicken.

For self-driving cars, we've already had the situation of human drivers playing games with self-driving cars at four-way stop signs. The human drivers aggressively do a rolling stop, and it has caused some self-driving cars to wait seemingly forever, since the self-driving car is programmed to not proceed until the other cars at the stop signs have come to a complete halt and waited their respective turn. Human drivers will be likely to play games with self-driving cars and the self-driving cars need to have better AI to handle these games. Likewise, the case for U-turns. If human drivers making U-turns are aware that a self-driving car can be conned into coming to halt to let the U-turn be made, those human drivers will likely edge out into the U-turn to trigger the self-driving car to come to a halt. This is something those human drivers would not have dared do with other human drivers.

In terms of a self-driving car executing a U-turn, it's a rather complex operation and therefore does need a specialized component of the AI to handle it.

Here are the major steps involved:

Planning for U-turn

The self-driving car needs to figure out when a U-turn makes sense to consider. Is it sensible to do a U-turn in the situation or would it be better to wait or do some other maneuver? Are the roadway conditions viable? And so on.

Pre-Positioning for the U-turn

The self-driving car needs to get itself into a posture that will allow for the U-turn. If the self-driving car is in the rightmost lanes and it needs to get over to a left turn lane, it will first need to make those lane changes to get over to the left turn slot. You likely see human drivers that miscalculate this and end-up screaming across lanes of traffic to reach the left turn slot, and in the process, disrupt and endanger other drivers. Don't want the self-driving car to do that.

U-turn Execution

After getting into the proper positioning for the U-turn, now the self-driving car will need to undertake the U-turn. Abandoning the U-turn is an option that also needs to be considered. If the U-turn itself now no longer seems possible, the self-driving car might be able to make just a left turn and deal with getting back onto track after that maneuver.

Post-Positioning after the U-turn

Once the U-turn has been executed, some human drivers will suddenly make a rapid right turn or try to get into other lanes of traffic. The self-driving car AI should have already during the planning stage have decided where it needs to be after the U-turn is completed and then navigate the car accordingly.

For our self-driving car AI software, it also keeps track of how mature the self-driving car is becoming at making U-turns. The more times it makes a U-turn, generally the better it gets, due to machine learning capabilities. Thus, there are some U-turns that at first it should not try, and then as it gets better, it can take on more complex U-turns.

On a related aspect, some say that by the use of neural networks that there is no need to actually "program" the AI to deal with U-turns. They assert that the self-driving car AI will simply gain awareness of U-turns and how to do them via having a large dataset of U-turns that it can pattern after. Though we agree that having the large data sets helps, it still does not overtake the need to have actual articulated strategies and tactics for doing U-turns. The AI of the self-driving car is not going to entirely be able to do U-turns by neural network or machine learning alone.

U-turns are a thing of beauty, when done right. Sometimes, there is not much judgement involved and it is a simple matter of following the roadway for a controlled and operated U-turn. In other situations, making a U-turn is an art. Self-driving cars are going to need to be able to do all of these kinds of U-turns, without which they would be inherently limited in their capabilities and not able to reach the vaunted Level 5 for self-driving cars. U-turns, love them or hate them, but either way the AI of a self-driving car should be versed in U-turns, knowing when, where, how, what, and the why of carrying out U-turns.

CHAPTER 19
SOFTWARE NEGLECT FOR SELF-DRIVING CARS

CHAPTER 19
SOFTWARE NEGLECT FOR SELF-DRIVING CARS

When last did your laptop, desktop computer, or smartphone encounter some kind of internal software glitch and it went to the blue screen of death (BSoD, or blue screen, as they call it), or in some other manner either halted working or automatically did a reboot on its own?

Happens all the time.

For those of you that are software developers, you likely already know that software can be quite brittle. It doesn't take much in terms of having your software code crash or falter, depending upon how well written or poorly written the code is. I've had some top-notch programmers that were sure their software could handle anything, and the next thing you know their beloved software hit a snag and did the wrong thing. If software is doing something that is relatively inconsequential and it happens to falter or crash, you can usually just restart the software or otherwise shrug off the difficulty it encountered.

This idea though of shrugging off a blue screen is not going to be sufficient for self-driving cars. Self-driving cars and the AI that runs them have to be right, else lives can be lost.

You don't want to be going along as an occupant in a self-driving car that is doing 70 miles per hour on the freeway and all of a sudden the system displays a message saying it has reached an untenable condition internally and needs to reboot. Even if somehow the system could do a reset in record time, the car would have proceeded forward at its breakneck speed and could very easily hit another car or careen off the road. In a Level 5 true self-driving car, most auto makers are removing any of the internal controls such as the steering wheel and pedals, thus, a human occupant could not takeover the wheel in such an emergency (though, even if the human could takeover the controls, it might already be too late in most such emergency circumstances).

In short, once we have Level 5 true self-driving cars, you are pretty much at the mercy of the software and AI that is guiding and directing the self-driving car. A recent survey by AIG of Americans found that about 75% said they didn't trust that a self-driving car could safely drive a car. Some pundits that are in favor of self-driving cars have ridiculed those 75% as being anti-technology and essentially Luddites. They are the unwashed. They are lacking in awareness of how great self-driving cars are.

For me, I would have actually thought that 100% would have said they don't trust a self-driving car to safely drive a car. The 25% that apparently expressed that it was safe, well, I don't think they know what's happening with self-driving cars. We are still a long ways from having a Level 5 true self-driving car – that's a self-driving car that can do anything that a human driver could do, and for which there is therefore no need and no provision to have a human drive the car. The self-driving cars that you keep hearing about and that are on the roads today are being accompanied by a specially trained back-up human driver as a just-in-case, and I assure you that the just-in-case is occurring aplenty.

The software that is being developed for self-driving cars is often being programmed by developers that have no experience in real-time control systems such as specialized systems that would be built to guide an airplane or a rocket ship. Though the developers might know the latest AI techniques and be seasoned software engineers, there are lots of tricky aspects about writing software that involves controlling a vehicle that is in motion, and that has the potential to be a hurtling moving object that can readily hurt or kill someone.

It's not just the programmers that cause some worry. The programming languages that they are using weren't particularly made for doing this kind of real-time systems programming. The tools they are using to develop and test the code aren't particularly made for this purpose either. They are also faced with incredibly tight deadlines, since the auto makers and tech companies are in an "arms race" to see who can get their self-driving car out into the market before the others. The assumption by the management and executives of these firms is that whomever gets there first, they will not only get the notoriety for it, but also will grab key market share and have a first-mover advantage that no other firm will be able to overtake.

It's a recipe for disaster.

There are many examples of software written for real-time motion oriented systems that have had terrible consequences due to a software glitch.

For example, the Ariane 5 rocket, in its Flight 501, has become known as one of the most famous or infamous examples of a software related glitch in a real-time motion oriented system. Upon launch in June 1996, the system encountered an internal integer overflow and had not been adequately designed and nor tested to deal with such a situation. The rocket then veered off its proper course. As it did so, the manner of its angle and speed began to cause the rocket to disintegrate. A self-destruct mechanism opted to terminate the flight and blow-up the rocket. Various estimates are that this cost about $370 million and could have been avoided if the software had better internal checks-and-balances.

They were lucky that there weren't any humans on-board the rocket. And, nor that any of the rocket parts that were destroyed midair came down and harmed any humans. When we hear about these cases of rockets exploding, we often don't think much about it since there is rarely human lives lost. The Mars Climate Orbiter robotic space probe struck the Mars atmosphere at the wrong angle due to some software issues and was destroyed. It was a $655 million dollar system. We usually just figure the insurance will cover it and don't otherwise give it much care. In this instance, the thrusters were supposed to be using newton-seconds but had instead gotten data in pound-seconds.

There was probably more outcry about Apple Maps than what we heard of concern about the preceding examples of software related glitches that had adverse outcomes. You might recall that in 2012, Apple opted to make use of Apple Maps rather than using Google Maps. Right away, people pointed out that lakes were missing or in the wrong place, train stations were missing or in the wrong place, bridges were missing or in the wrong place, etc. This was quite a snafu at the time. If you go back in history to 1993, some of you might remember that Intel's Pentium chip was discovered to have had a math error in it, which could mess-up certain kinds of division calculations (it was the FDIV). This ended-up costing Intel about $475 million to fix and replace.

All of these kinds of software and system related glitches and problems are likely to surface in self-driving cars. The AI and systems of self-driving cars are complex. There are lots and lots of components. Many of the components are developed by a various parties and then brought together into one presumably cohesive system. It is a good bet that not each of these components is written to absolutely avoid any glitches. It is a good bet that when these systems are combined together that something will go awry of one component trying to communicate with another component.

In case you are doubtful about my claims, you ought to take a close look at the open source software that is being made available for self-driving cars.

At the Cybernetic Self-Driving Car Institute, we have been using this open source software in our self-driving car AI systems, and also finding lots of software glitches or issues that others might not realize are sitting in there and will be like a time-bomb ready to implode at the worst times when incorporated into an auto makers self-driving car system.

Here are the kinds of issues that we've been discovering and then making sure that our AI self-driving car software is properly written to catch or avoid:

Integer Overflow

In self-driving car software, there are lots of calculations that involve figuring out the needed feeds to the controls of the car, such as the angle of the car and throttle indications. It is very easy for these calculations to throw off an integer overflow condition. Most of the open source has no detection for an integer overflow. In some cases, there is detection, but then the follow-up action by the code doesn't make any sense in that if the code was truly in the middle of a crucial calculation controlling the car, the error catch code merely does a reset to zero or some other simplistic operation. This will be dangerous and could have very adverse consequences.

Buffer Overflow

The self-driving software code sets up say a table of 100 indexed items. At run-time, the software goes past the 100 and tries to access the 105th element of the table. In some programming languages, this is automatically caught at run-time, but in others it is not. This is one of the most common exploits for cyberattacks. In any case, in code that is running a self-driving car, having a buffer overflow can lead to dire results. Code that checks for a buffer overflow has to also be shrewd enough to know what to do when the condition occurs. Detecting it is insufficient, and the code needs to also take recovery action that makes sense for the context of the buffer overflow that occurs.

Date/Time Stamps

Much of what happens in the real-time efforts of self-driving cars involves activities occurring over time. It is vital that an instruction being sent to the controls of the car have a date/time stamp, which then if multiple instructions arrive, the receiving system can figure out in what order the instructions were sent. We've seen few of the open source software deal with this. Those that do deal with it are not well using date/time stamps and seem to be unaware of the importance of their use.

Magical Numbers

Some of the open source code is written toward a particular make and model of a car. And likewise a particular make and model of sensory devices. Within the code, the programmers are putting so-called magical numbers. For example, suppose a particular LIDAR sensor gets a code of 185482 which means to refresh, and so the software sends that number to the LIDAR sensor. But, other programmers that come along to reuse the code aren't aware that the 185482 is specific to that make and model, and assume they can use the code for some other LIDAR device. The use of magical numbers is a lousy programming technique and should not be encouraged. Unfortunately, programmers under the gun to get code done are apt to use magical numbers.

Error Checking

Much of the open source software for self-driving cars has meager if any true error checking. Developing error checking code is time consuming and "slows" down the effort to develop software, at least that's the view of many. For a real-time motion oriented system of a self-driving car, that kind of mindset has to be rectified. You have to include error checking. Very extensive and robust error checking. Some auto makers and their software engineering groups are handing over the error checking to the junior programmers, figuring that it is wasted effort for the senior developers. All I can say is that when errors within the code arise during actual use, and if the error checking code is naïve and simplistic, it's ultimately going to backfire on those firms that opted to treat error checking as something unimportant and merely an aside.

For our code that we are developing for self-driving cars, we insist on in-depth error checking. We force our developers into considering all the variants of what can go wrong. We use the technique of having walk-through's of the code to try and have other eyes be able to spot errors that might arise. We make use of separate Quality Assurance (QA) teams to double and triple check code. And, we at times use the technique of having multiple versions of the same code. This can provide for situations wherein if one version hiccups during real-time use, the other version which is also running at the same time can be turned to as a back-up to continue running.

Any code that we don't write ourselves, we put through an equally stringent examination. Of course, one problem is that many of the allied software components are made available only as executables. This means that we cannot inspect their source code to see how well it is written and what provisions it has for error checking. Self-driving cars are at the whim of those other components. We try to surround those components with our software such that if the component falters that our master software can try to detect and takeover, but even this is difficult if not problematic in many circumstances.

There is a rising notion in the software industry of referring to software that has these kinds of failings of error checking to be considered instances of software neglect.

In other words, it is the developers that neglected to appropriately prepare the software to catch and handle internal error conditions. The software neglects to detect and remedy these aspects. I like this way of expressing it, since otherwise there is an implication that no one is held accountable for software glitches. When someone says that a piece of software had an error, such as the Ariane 5 rocket that faltered due to an integer overflow, it is easy to just raise your hands in the air and say that's the way the software code bounces. Nobody is at fault. It just happens.

Instead, by describing it as software neglect, right away people begin to ask questions such as how and why was it neglected? They would be right to ask such questions. When self-driving cars begin to exhibit problems on our roadways, we cannot just shrug our shoulders and pretend that computers will be computers. We cannot accept the idea that the blue screen on a self-driving car is understandable since we get it on our laptops, desktops, and smartphones. These errors arise and are not caught by software due to the software being poorly written. It is software that had insufficient attention devoted to getting it right.

I realize that some software developers will counter argue that you can never know that software will always work correctly. There is no means to prove that software will work as intended across all situations and circumstances. Yes, I realize that aspect. But, this is also a bit of a ruse or screen. This is a clever ploy to then say that well if we cannot be perfect in detecting and dealing with errors, we can then get away with doing the minimum required, or even maybe not checking at all. That's a false way to think about the matter. Not being able to be perfect does not give carte blanche to being imperfect in whatever ways you want.

In 1991, a United States Patriot missile system failed to detect an incoming missile attack on an army barracks. The tracking system had an inaccurate calculating piece of code, and the calculation got worse the longer the system was being operated without a reboot. This particular system had been going for an estimated 100 hours or longer. The internal software was not ready for this lengthy of a run, and so variables in the code were getting off, a little bit with each passing hour. As a result, the Patriot system was looking in the wrong place and was not able to shoot at the incoming missiles.

The estimated cost for the Patriot system, covering its development and ongoing maintenance, has been pegged around at least $125 billion dollars or more.

Meanwhile, you might have recently seen that it was inadvertently revealed that Google has spent around $1.1 billion on its so far six-year "Project Chauffeur" effort (essentially their self-driving car project). This number was found in a deposition involving the lawsuit between Waymo and Uber. It had not been previously disclosed by Google.

Why do I point this out?

Some people gasped at the one billion dollars of Google and thought it was a huge number. I say it is a tiny number. I am not directly comparing the spending to the Patriot system, but the point I was trying to make is that the Patriot system has its flaws and yet billions upon billions of dollars have been spent on it. In my opinion, we need to spend a lot more on self-driving car development.

If we truly want a safe self-driving car, we need to make sure that it does not suffer from software neglect. To properly avert software neglect, it takes a lot of developers, development tools, and attention, including and especially to the error checking aspects. In the movie Jaws, there is a famous quote that they needed a bigger boat – in the field of AI self-driving cars, we need a bigger budget. We are underspending for AI self-driving software and yet setting very high expectations.

APPENDIX

APPENDIX A
TEACHING WITH THIS MATERIAL

The material in this book can be readily used either as a supplemental to other content for a class, or it can also be used as a core set of textbook material for a specialized class. Classes where this material is most likely used include any classes at the college or university level that want to augment the class by offering thought provoking and educational essays about AI and self-driving cars.

In particular, here are some aspects for class use:

o <u>Computer Science</u>. Studying AI, autonomous vehicles, etc.

o <u>Business</u>. Exploring technology and it adoption for business.

o <u>Sociology</u>. Sociological views on the adoption and advancement of technology.

Specialized classes at the undergraduate and graduate level can also make use of this material.

For each chapter, consider whether you think the chapter provides material relevant to your course topic. There is plenty of opportunity to get the students thinking about the topic and force them to decide whether they agree or disagree with the points offered and positions taken. I would also encourage you to have the students do additional research beyond the chapter material presented (I provide next some suggested assignments they can do).

RESEARCH ASSIGNMENTS ON THESE TOPICS

Your students can find background material on these topics, doing so in various business and technical publications. I list below the top ranked AI related journals. For business publications, I would suggest the usual culprits such as the Harvard Business Review, Forbes, Fortune, WSJ, and the like.

Here are some suggestions of homework or projects that you could assign to students:

a) <u>Assignment for foundational AI research topic</u>: Research and prepare a paper and a presentation on a specific aspect of Deep AI, Machine Learning, ANN, etc. The paper should cite at least 3 reputable sources. Compare and contrast to what has been stated in this book.

b) <u>Assignment for the Self-Driving Car topic</u>: Research and prepare a paper and Self-Driving Cars. Cite at least 3 reputable sources and analyze the characterizations. Compare and contrast to what has been stated in this book.

c) <u>Assignment for a Business topic</u>: Research and prepare a paper and a presentation on businesses and advanced technology. What is hot, and what is not? Cite at least 3 reputable sources. Compare and contrast to the depictions in this book.

d) <u>Assignment to do a Startup:</u> Have the students prepare a paper about how they might startup a business in this realm. They must submit a sound Business Plan for the startup. They could also be asked to present their Business Plan and so should also have a presentation deck to coincide with it.

You can certainly adjust the aforementioned assignments to fit to your particular needs and the class structure. You'll notice that I ask for 3 reputable cited sources for the paper writing based assignments. I usually steer students toward "reputable" publications, since otherwise they will cite some oddball source that has no credentials other than that they happened to write something and post it onto the Internet. You can define "reputable" in whatever way you prefer, for example some faculty think Wikipedia is not reputable while others believe it is reputable and allow students to cite it.

The reason that I usually ask for at least 3 citations is that if the student only does one or two citations they usually settle on whatever they happened to find the fastest. By requiring three citations, it usually seems to force them to look around, explore, and end-up probably finding five or more, and then whittling it down to 3 that they will actually use.

I have not specified the length of their papers, and leave that to you to tell the students what you prefer. For each of those assignments, you could end-up with a short one to two pager, or you could do a dissertation length paper. Base the length on whatever best fits for your class, and the credit amount of the assignment within the context of the other grading metrics you'll be using for the class.

I mention in the assignments that they are to do a paper and prepare a presentation. I usually try to get students to present their work. This is a good practice for what they will do in the business world. Most of the time, they will be required to prepare an analysis and present it. If you don't have the class time or inclination to have the students present, then you can of course cut out the aspect of them putting together a presentation.

If you want to point students toward highly ranked journals in AI, here's a list of the top journals as reported by *various citation counts sources* (this list changes year to year):

- o Communications of the ACM
- o Artificial Intelligence
- o Cognitive Science
- o IEEE Transactions on Pattern Analysis and Machine Intelligence
- o Foundations and Trends in Machine Learning
- o Journal of Memory and Language
- o Cognitive Psychology
- o Neural Networks
- o IEEE Transactions on Neural Networks and Learning Systems
- o IEEE Intelligent Systems
- o Knowledge-based Systems

GUIDE TO USING THE CHAPTERS

For each of the chapters, I provide next some various ways to use the chapter material. You can assign the tasks as individual homework assignments, or the tasks can be used with team projects for the class. You can easily layout a series of assignments, such as indicating that the students are to do item "a" below for say Chapter 1, then "b" for the next chapter of the book, and so on.

a) What is the main point of the chapter and describe in your own words the significance of the topic,

b) Identify at least two aspects in the chapter that you agree with, and support your concurrence by providing at least one other outside researched item as support; make sure to explain your basis for disagreeing with the aspects,

c) Identify at least two aspects in the chapter that you disagree with, and support your disagreement by providing at least one other outside researched item as support; make sure to explain your basis for disagreeing with the aspects,

d) Find an aspect that was not covered in the chapter, doing so by conducting outside research, and then explain how that aspect ties into the chapter and what significance it brings to the topic,

e) Interview a specialist in industry about the topic of the chapter, collect from them their thoughts and opinions, and readdress the chapter by citing your source and how they compared and contrasted to the material,

f) Interview a relevant academic professor or researcher in a college or university about the topic of the chapter, collect from them their thoughts and opinions, and readdress the chapter by citing your source and how they compared and contrasted to the material,

g) Try to update a chapter by finding out the latest on the topic, and ascertain whether the issue or topic has now been solved or whether it is still being addressed, explain what you come up with.

The above are all ways in which you can get the students of your class involved in considering the material of a given chapter. You could mix things up by having one of those above assignments per each week, covering the chapters over the course of the semester or quarter.

NEW ADVANCES IN AI AUTONOMOUS DRIVERLESS SELF-DRIVING CARS

As a reminder, here are the chapters of the book and you can select whichever chapters you find most valued for your particular class:

<u>Chapter Title</u>

1. Eliot Framework for AI Self-Driving Cars
2. Self-Driving Cars Learning from Self-Driving Cars
3. Imitation as Deep Learning for Self-Driving Cars
4. Assessing Federal Regulations for Self-Driving Cars
5. Bandwagon Effect for Self-Driving Cars
6. AI Backdoor Security Holes for Self-Driving Cars
7. Debiasing of AI for Self-Driving Cars
8. Algorithmic Transparency for Self-Driving Cars
9. Motorcycle Disentanglement for Self-Driving Cars
10. Graceful Degradation Handling of Self-Driving Cars
11. AI for Home Garage Parking of Self-Driving Cars
12. Motivational AI Irrationality for Self-Driving Cars
13. Curiosity as Cognition for Self-Driving Cars
14. Automotive Recalls of Self-Driving Cars
15. Internationalizing AI for Self-Driving Cars
16. Sleeping as AI Mechanism for Self-Driving Cars
17. Car Insurance Scams and Self-Driving Cars
18. U-Turn Traversal AI for Self-Driving Cars
19. Software Neglect for Self-Driving Cars

Lance B. Eliot

Companion Book By This Author

Advances in AI and Autonomous Vehicles: Cybernetic Self-Driving Cars

Practical Advances in Artificial Intelligence (AI) and Machine Learning

by

Dr. Lance B. Eliot, MBA, PhD

Chapter Title
1. Genetic Algorithms for Self-Driving Cars
2. Blockchain for Self-Driving Cars
3. Machine Learning and Data for Self-Driving Cars
4. Edge Problems at Core of True Self-Driving Cars
5. Solving the Roundabout Traversal Problem for SD Cars
6. Parallel Parking Mindless Task for SD Cars: Step It Up
7. Caveats of Open Source for Self-Driving Cars
8. Catastrophic Cyber Hacking of Self-Driving Cars
9. Conspicuity for Self-Driving Cars
10. Accident Scene Traversal for Self-Driving Cars
11. Emergency Vehicle Awareness for Self-Driving Cars
12. Are Left Turns Right for Self-Driving Cars
13. Going Blind: When Sensors Fail on Self-Driving Cars
14. Roadway Debris Cognition for Self-Driving Cars
15. Avoiding Pedestrian Roadkill by Self-Driving Cars
16. When Accidents Happen to Self-Driving Cars
17. Illegal Driving for Self-Driving Cars
18. Making AI Sense of Road Signs
19. Parking Your Car the AI Way
20. Not Fast Enough: Human Factors in Self-Driving Cars
21. State of Government Reporting on Self-Driving Cars
22. The Head Nod Problem for Self-Driving Cars
23. CES Reveals Self-Driving Car Differences

This title is available via Amazon and other book sellers

Companion Book By This Author

Self-Driving Cars:
"The Mother of All AI Projects"

by Dr. Lance B. Eliot, MBA, PhD

Chapter Title

1. Grand Convergence Explains Rise of Self-Driving Cars
2. Here is Why We Need to Call Them Self-Driving Cars
3. Richter Scale for Levels of Self-Driving Cars
4. LIDAR as Secret Sauce for Self-Driving Cars
5. Pied Piper Approach to SD Car-Following
6. Sizzle Reel Trickery for AI Self-Driving Car Hype
7. Roller Coaster Public Perception of Self-Driving Cars
8. Brainless Self-Driving Shuttles Not Same as SD Cars
9. First Salvo Class Action Lawsuits for Defective SD Cars
10. AI Fake News About Self-Driving Cars
11. Rancorous Ranking of Self-Driving Cars
12. Product Liability for Self-Driving Cars
13. Humans Colliding with Self-Driving Cars
14. Elderly Boon or Bust for Self-Driving Cars
15. Simulations for Self-Driving Cars: Machine Learning
16. DUI Drunk Driving by Self-Driving Cars
17. Ten Human-Driving Foibles: Deep Learning
18. Art of Defensive Driving is Key to Self-Driving Cars
19. Cyclops Approach to AI Self-Driving Cars is Myopic
20. Steering Wheel Gets Self-Driving Car Attention
21. Remote Piloting is a Self-Driving Car Crutch
22. Self-Driving Cars: Zero Fatalities, Zero Chance
23. Goldrush: Self-Driving Car Lawsuit Bonanza Ahead
24. Road Trip Trickery for Self-Driving Trucks and Cars
25. Ethically Ambiguous Self-Driving Car

This title is available via Amazon and other book sellers

Companion Book By This Author

***Innovation and Thought Leadership
on Self-Driving Driverless Cars***

by Dr. Lance B. Eliot, MBA, PhD

<u>Chapter Title</u>

1. Sensor Fusion for Self-Driving Cars
2. Street Scene Free Space Detection Self-Driving Cars
3. Self-Awareness for Self-Driving Cars
4. Cartographic Trade-offs for Self-Driving Cars
5. Toll Road Traversal for Self-Driving Cars
6. Predictive Scenario Modeling for Self-Driving Cars
7. Selfishness for Self-Driving Cars
8. Leap Frog Driving for Self-Driving Cars
9. Proprioceptive IMU's for Self-Driving Cars
10. Robojacking of Self-Driving Cars
11. Self-Driving Car Moonshot and Mother of AI Projects
12. Marketing of Self-Driving Cars
13. Are Airplane Autopilots Same as Self-Driving Cars
14. Savvy Self-Driving Car Regulators: Marc Berman
15. Event Data Recorders (EDR) for Self-Driving Cars
16. Looking Behind You for Self-Driving Cars
17. In-Car Voice Commands NLP for Self-Driving Cars
18. When Self-Driving Cars Get Pulled Over by a Cop
19. Brainjacking Neuroprosthetus Self-Driving Cars

This title is available via Amazon and other book sellers

Lance B. Eliot

ABOUT THE AUTHOR

Dr. Lance B. Eliot, MBA, PhD is the CEO of Techbruim, Inc. and Executive Director of the Cybernetic Self-Driving Car Institute, and has over twenty years of industry experience including serving as a corporate officer in a billion dollar firm and was a Partner in a major executive services firm. He is also a serial entrepreneur having founded, ran, and sold several high-tech related businesses. He previously hosted the popular radio show *Technotrends* that was also available on American Airlines flights via their in-flight audio program. Author or co-author of a dozen books and over 300 articles, he has made appearances on CNN, and has been a frequent speaker at industry conferences.

A former professor at the University of Southern California (USC), he founded and led an innovative research lab on Artificial Intelligence in Business. Known as the "AI Insider" his writings on AI advances and trends has been widely read and cited. He also previously served on the faculty of the University of California Los Angeles (UCLA), and was a visiting professor at other major universities. He was elected to the International Board of the Society for Information Management (SIM), a prestigious association of over 3,000 high-tech executives worldwide.

He has performed extensive community service, including serving as Senior Science Adviser to the Vice Chair of the Congressional Committee on Science & Technology. He has served on the Board of the OC Science & Engineering Fair (OCSEF), where he is also has been a Grand Sweepstakes judge, and likewise served as a judge for the Intel International SEF (ISEF). He served as the Vice Chair of the Association for Computing Machinery (ACM) Chapter, a prestigious association of computer scientists. Dr. Eliot has been a shark tank judge for the USC Mark Stevens Center for Innovation on start-up pitch competitions, and served as a mentor for several incubators and accelerators in Silicon Valley and Silicon Beach. He served on several Boards and Committees at USC, including having served on the Marshall Alumni Association (MAA) Board in Southern California.

Dr. Eliot holds a PhD from USC, MBA, and Bachelor's in Computer Science, and earned the CDP, CCP, CSP, CDE, and CISA certifications. Born and raised in Southern California, and having traveled and lived internationally, he enjoys scuba diving, surfing, and sailing.

Lance B. Eliot

ADDENDUM

New Advances in AI Autonomous Driverless Self-Driving Cars

Practical Advances in Artificial Intelligence (AI) and Machine Learning

By
Dr. Lance B. Eliot, MBA, PhD

For supplemental materials of this book, visit:
www.lance-blog.com

For special orders of this book, contact:
LBE Press Publishing
Email: LBE.Press.Publishing@gmail.com

Made in the USA
Middletown, DE
18 May 2018